CACTI AND SUCCULENTS

■ Step-by-Step to Growing Success ■

Bill Keen

CROWOOD GARDENING GUIDES

First published in 1990 by
The Crowood Press
Ramsbury, Marlborough,
Wiltshire SN8 2HE

British Library Cataloguing in Publication Data

Keen, W. C.
Cacti and succulents.
I. Cacti. Cultivation
I. Title
635.9'3347

ISBN 1 85223 264 1

Picture Credits

All photographs by the author, except Figs 13,14,15,33,34,35,36,37 and the front cover by Dave Pike.
Colour artwork by Claire Upsdale-Jones.

The photograph on page 4 shows *Thelocactus bicolor*.

Dedication

To my parents, who encouraged my early enthusiasm for these wonderful plants, and my wife Pauline for her patience when it became an obsession.

Typeset by Avonset, Midsomer Norton, Bath. Printed and bound by Times Publishing Group, Singapore.

Contents

CHAPTER 1

The World of Cacti and Succulents

ATTRACTIONS

Succulent plants have been a feature of the horticultural scene for a long time, yet their appeal has not been dimmed by the passing years. When first brought into cultivation, their exotic appearance made them objects of great curiosity. Contemporary accounts reveal the sense of wonderment induced in the minds of those acquainted only with the familiar garden plants of the day. The first flowering of some of those early introductions was often deemed newsworthy but then, as now, the press reports were sometimes greatly distorted.

Films and television have made the plants more familiar today. They are freely available from garden centres and chainstores, and one might assume that they would no longer retain their fascination. Yet one has only to watch the reaction of children at a flower show to realise that there is something elemental about the attractions of the plants. The children will pass magnificent displays of roses, chrysanthemums and the like with scarcely a glance, but very few will fail to linger in front of a display of succulent plants.

What is it about these plants that appeals? It is usually cacti that make the initial impact. Their appearance is so different from that of other plants that attention is drawn to them. Instead of slender leafy stems, the majority of cacti have swollen stems with spines taking the place of leaves. The association of the plants with a struggle for life in a hostile environment enhances their appeal. The climax comes when the first flowering cactus is seen. Cactus flowers have a delicate beauty which contrasts with the stark appearance of the plants, and they are often brightly coloured.

The range of forms among the cacti is considerable. Hollywood has made everyone familiar with the columnar 'organ pipe' and flat-padded 'prickly pear' types, but there are also cacti with globular bodies and many which offset to form mounds of clustering stems. In size they range from tiny plants with bodies less that ½in (1cm) in diameter to giants 40ft (12m) or more in height.

In addition to the cacti, many other plants have evolved to survive in arid regions. Some have an appearance superficially similar to that of the cacti, with fleshy stems and an absence of leaves. Some are rosette plants with fleshy leaves, while others compromise by having stout moisture-retaining stems and deciduous non-fleshy leaves. The variety of forms among these is even greater than among the cacti. Add the fact that many of the leaves are of delicate pastel colours, or covered with a powdery farina, or clad with soft hairs just appealing to be stroked, and one can understand why people find it difficult to resist touching the plants.

The exotic appearance of these plants might lead the uninitiated to think that they are difficult to cultivate. This is not the case: they are among the easiest of plants to grow. Apart from a small number, which are best avoided until experience has been gained by growing a variety of types,

Fig 1 Weingartia corroana.

cacti and succulents are undemanding in their requirements. Given a porous compost, a position in good light, moderate watering and enough warmth to maintain a temperature just above freezing point, the majority can be expected not only to survive but to flourish and flower. It is possible to grow fine specimens on a windowsill, though a greenhouse makes life easier for the plants and their owner. Having evolved to cope with the rigours of a harsh natural environment, the plants are forgiving of neglect. A plant that can survive months of drought in the wild will not take exception to lack of watering while its owner is away on holiday.

DISTINCTION BETWEEN CACTI AND OTHER SUCCULENTS

The phrase 'cacti and succulents' has been in use for so long that it would be optimistic to expect that clarification would lead to adoption of a more logical term. It is, however, rather nonsensical since all cacti are succulents: it is akin to using a term 'dogs and quadrupeds'.

The issue is further confused by the difficulty of defining the term 'succulent'. To the layman, a succulent is a fleshy plant, but there are degrees of succulence and a 'grey' area between the truly succulent and completely non-succulent plants. Since many of these borderline plants are highly regarded by collectors, a blind eye is often turned to their physical attributes and they are accepted as succulent.

It is easier to define a cactus: as a member of the botanical family Cactaceae. What then are the features that delimit this family? Possession of a fleshy stem and spines is not enough: some of the other succulents have evolved in a similar manner to cope with the same type of environment. It is likely, however, that a plant with a fleshy stem and spines is a cactus. Confirmation is obtained by studying the origin of the spines. If they emerge from a small pad-like structure, the

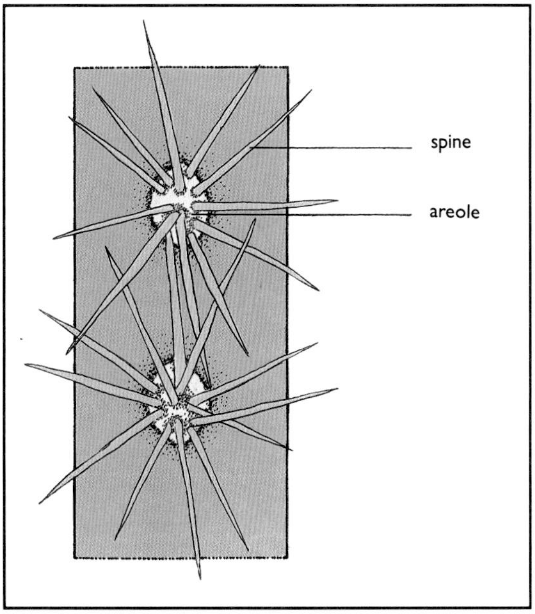

Fig 2 It is the areole that distinguishes cacti from other succulents.

plant is a cactus. The pad-like structure is called an areole, and it is this feature that distinguishes the cacti. Just to confuse the picture further, some cacti do not possess spines and the areoles are minute and difficult to recognise. The familiar 'Christmas Cactus' falls into this category, but is a true cactus for all that.

CLASSIFICATION AND NOMENCLATURE

One of the aspects of building a collection of succulent plants that bedevils the newcomer is the perceived difficulty of coping with botanical names. At first sight, scientific names often appear impossible to spell, pronounce or remember. It is tempting to think that, if the plants were given popular names, life would be much simpler for the collector.

Sadly, this is not so, though periodically efforts have been made to popularise common names.

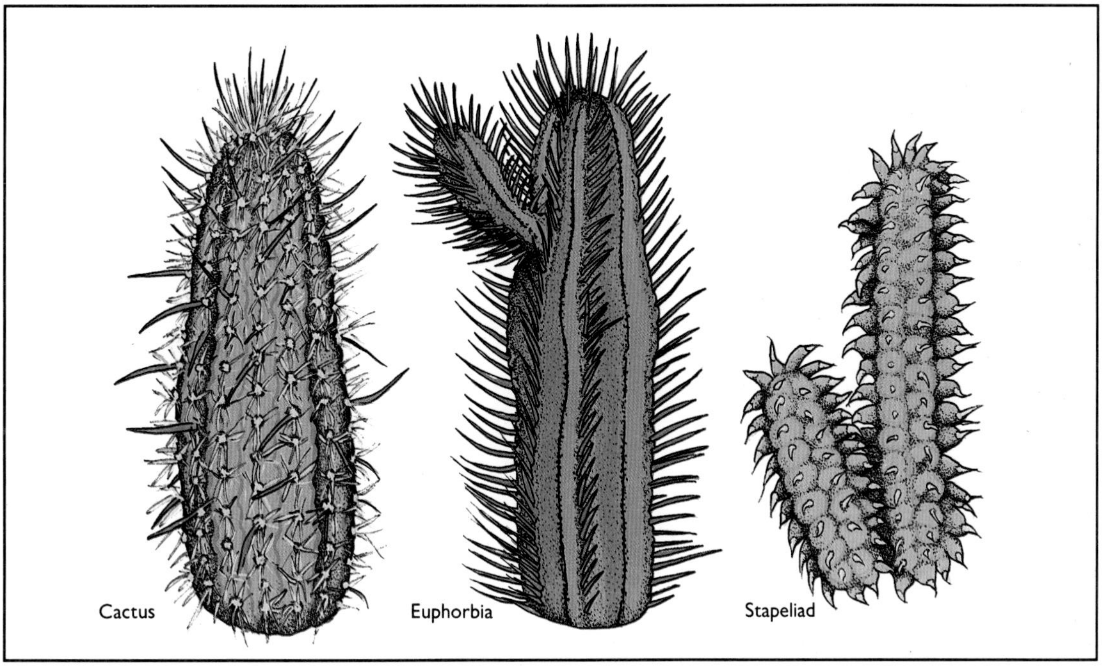

Fig 3 Three types of succulents.

These attempts inevitably fail, as they lead to ambiguity. In many cases the same plant has been given several popular names. For example the familiar houseplant *Aloe variegata* has been given the popular names 'Partridge Breast Aloe', 'Tiger Aloe', 'Zebra Aloe' and 'Mackerel Plant' among others. On the other hand, different plants have been given the same popular name. For example, both the epiphytic *Aporocactus flagelliformis*, with slender trailing stems, and the globular *Pediocactus simpsonii* have been given the popular name 'Snake Cactus'. Although popular names are often descriptive of the plant, many are not: what, for example, is to be made of 'Red-headed Irishman' for *Mammillaria spinosissima*? Try asking for that in a garden centre!

An unambiguous system of identifying plants (and animals) was proposed by Linnaeus in the eighteenth century and has since become the standard. This is the binomial system, which uses a generic name followed by a specific epithet as a unique identifier. As the names are based (in the majority of cases) on the 'dead' classical languages Latin and Greek, they are unaffected by the changes in meaning that occur as 'live' languages develop. This makes the system equally acceptable in all parts of the world.

In the binomial system, closely related plants are grouped in a *genus* and all carry the same generic name, for example *Mammillaria*. They are distinguished from one another by being given different specific epithets, for example *elongata* and *prolifera*. Thus *Mammillaria elongata*, a cactus with long finger-like stems, is distinguished from the related *Mammillaria prolifera* which offsets freely to form a large cluster of globular bodies.

Man delights in classifying the surrounding world, and the science of fitting the natural world

Fig 4 Mammillaria schiedeana

into convenient pigeon-holes is called 'taxonomy'. The botanical taxonomist aims to produce an acceptable 'family tree' defining the relationships between the various kinds of plant. Mention has been made of the genus, the group of closely related plants. The division of the group into recognisably different kinds leads to the category of *species*. In some cases the differences between two or more kinds may be very small, perhaps no more than a variation in flower colour, and the taxonomist may distinguish them as *varieties* of a single species. Moving in the other direction, related genera may be grouped into a botanical *Family*. There are other levels of distinction used by the taxonomist, but these need not concern the novice.

Plants receive their names for a variety of reasons, and effort expended on learning the meaning of a name is well spent (it does not involve spending hours poring over a Latin grammar). The specific epithets in particular often relate to obvious features of the plants. Some names, for instance, are based on colour: they may be applied to the colour of the body, the spination or the flowers. Another group relates to size and shape and may be applied to the whole plant or some feature such as the leaves. Sometimes two such terms may be combined to produce a name that is almost a short description, for example *longispinus* meaning long-spined or *aureiflorus* meaning golden-flowered.

There are other epithets which give a clue to the localities where the plants grow. Some of these are based on place-names which may be the names of countries or much smaller geographical units such as mountains or villages. Another group relates to the natural habitat, describing the terrain in which the plants are found. A knowledge of the meanings of these names may provide hints to aid successful cultivation.

When it comes to the pronunciation of plant names, such rules as there are tend to be flouted. Perhaps the best advice to novices is to listen carefully to the manner in which more experienced collectors pronounce the names.

Fig 5 Echinocereus pectinatus v. dasyacanthus.

They may not be strictly correct, but usually reflect common usage. Although sometimes forbidding at first sight, the names of succulent plants are as simple to cope with as those of such popular garden plants as antirrhinum and chrysanthemum!

GEOGRAPHICAL DISTRIBUTION

If one rejects the concept of spontaneous creation of a wide range of plant forms that remain fixed for all time, one is led to the concept of gradual evolution. It is now generally accepted that the earth has undergone many changes during its long existence. The principal land masses, which formed as the new planet cooled, gradually separated and drifted to their present positions. Accompanying the geographical changes, there have been climatic changes.

Plants evolved from the simplest algae by a slow process of adaptation and mutation. As climatic conditions changed, areas of aridity developed. Plants unsuited to the new conditions died out, but occasionally a few specimens possessed some characteristic, perhaps slightly fleshy leaves, which enabled them to survive. Sometimes the progeny of these survivors also possessed the required characteristic, and over many generations the original type evolved into a slightly different form better suited to the changed environment. Occasionally mutation, an abrupt change in some characteristic, occurred. Usually the changed character gave the plant no advantage and the mutant died out with its fellows, but every so often a mutation was beneficial and succeeding generations inherited the desirable characteristic. Gradually, over many millions of years, new types of plant evolved and set about colonising their surroundings.

Cacti are native to the Americas. There are a few species of *Rhipsalis*, a genus of epiphytes otherwise confined to the New World, which are found in Africa and Madagascar, apparently as native plants. There has been much speculation on this point. Were the plants already in existence before the land masses that became Africa and South America separated, and therefore left to develop in parallel with their transatlantic relatives? Did the plants evolve from different ancestors so that present similarities which place them in the same genus can be attributed to chance? Have seeds been transported across the Atlantic Ocean by some agency such as birds? Did sailors in ancient times carry fragments of plant material with them? Probably the puzzle will never be solved.

Some cacti have been carried by man to other parts of the world, for a variety of reasons. Where conditions have been favourable, the plants have often become a feature of the landscape. Travellers in the countries bordering the Mediterranean Sea will have seen 'prickly pears' apparently growing wild, but these are in fact only naturalised. The 'prickly pear' was also introduced into southern Africa and Australia as potential food for cattle during the dry season. In Queensland, in particular, the cactus found con-

Fig 6 Rebutia minuscula.

ditions so much to its liking that it spread rapidly and became a serious problem. As it regenerated quickly from small fragments of stem, eradication by cutting, ploughing and fire proved impossible. Only by introducing an insect pest specific to the cactus was the infestation brought under control.

Within the Americas, cacti are found from the Canadian prairies to the Argentinian pampas. Apart from those occurring on islands close to the mainland, cacti are also found in the West Indies and on the Galápagos Islands. The greatest concentrations occur in the most arid regions. There competition from other plants and predation by animals are less and cacti may become the dominant feature of the vegetation. In the northern part of the continent, the deserts of the south-western states of the USA adjoining Mexico are home to a large number of cacti.

In South America, the vast area of the rain-forest is unsuitable for terrestrial cacti, though a number of epiphytic types grow there. To the west of the Andean mountain chain which runs down the western side of the continent is a narrow strip comprising Chile and Peru. This area is affected by the Humboldt current of the Pacific Ocean, flowing northwards along the coast. It is an interesting region, almost rainless, where the only moisture available is in the form of coastal mist. Here are found several genera of cacti.

On the eastern side of the Andes and in the northern part of the subcontinent lies the great bulk of the Amazon rain-forest, which provides a natural barrier separating the terrestrial cacti of the northern hemisphere from those of South America. South of the rain-forest there are drier regions where a great diversity of cacti has evolved. The south-eastern part of Brazil possesses a rich cactus flora. So too do the neighbouring countries, Paraguay and Uruguay. The greatest concentration, however, occurs nearer to the Andean chain in north-western Argentina and Bolivia. The plants of these areas range from columnar types that are dominant features of the landscape to small plants growing among grass and scrub.

Although the Andes serve as a barrier separating the eastern species from those of the west, they also provide a habitat that has been exploited by other cacti. On the high plateaux between the main ranges, at altitudes up to 15,000ft (4,500m) where the night-time temperature may fall to −5 °F (−20 °C), a wide range of cacti have made their home. The area may receive no precipitation for three-quarters of the year and this, coupled with day-time temperatures up to 70 °F (20 °C) makes it unsuitable for most other plants.

The other succulents are more widespread than the cacti, and can be found in all parts of the world. It often surprises people to learn that succulent plants can be found in Siberia, but *Orostachys spinosus* grows there. Even more surprisingly, the great deserts of the world, the Sahara, the Arabian and the Australian deserts, support very few succulents.

The most important area for succulents comprises the southern and eastern parts of the African continent. The geography and climate show many parallels with those of the Americas. For example, on the western side of the continent is found the Namib Desert. Like the Atacama Desert of Chile, this is an extremely arid region, receiving less than ⅔in (15mm) of rain a year. Offshore the cold Benguela current causes coastal mists which roll inland, enabling drought-tolerant plants to survive. Elsewhere there are high mountains, though not so high as the Andes, which provide specialised habitats for succulents that can withstand occasional sub-zero temperatures.

In recent years Madagascar has yielded many of its treasures which, although often more demanding than other succulents in their requirements, have become very popular with collectors. The Horn of Africa and the southern part of the Arabian subcontinent are other areas that have been explored recently and are still producing new species.

It should not be thought that cacti are the only succulent plants to be found in the Americas. The same conditions that led to their evolution

Fig 7 Umbilicus rupestris.

have caused members of other botanical families to adapt. It is a little surprising that the succulents found in the Americas have, in general, adapted in a different manner to the cacti. Whereas the cacti are stem-succulents, most of the American succulents are leaf-succulents. One might have expected that some plant families would have developed swollen stems similar to those of the cacti.

Those who live in Britain are inured to its damp climate, which is scarcely conducive to the growth of succulent plants. Yet there are places, such as exposed rock-faces, where the rain does not penetrate to any depth but rapidly drains away. These situations provide a suitable environment for a succulent flora comprising a few members of the family Crassulaceae. Man has also had an influence on the distribution of these native succulents. When walls were built to enclose fields, suitable habitats were created for the plants, and these were soon colonised.

Mention has been made of the 'prickly pear' being taken to distant parts of the world for use as cattle feed. The desire to enhance our surroundings leads to the transplanting of many plants, and explains why cacti can be encountered in the Mediterranean area and elsewhere. Belief in their medicinal properties, real or imagined, has also led people to carry plants with them on their migrations.

CLIMATIC CONDITIONS AND ADAPTATION

The major problems facing any plant in an arid environment are those of obtaining and retaining the water necessary for existence. In many desert habitats the annual precipitation in the form of rain or snow is very low. The most arid areas receive only a few millimetres of rain annually. Elsewhere the precipitation is greater, up to 8in (200mm) a year, but this upper limit is only one-third of that enjoyed by London. Often the whole of the annual supply of moisture is deposited during a wet season of a few weeks which is followed by a dry season of many months. Sometimes the life-giving water must be acquired from mists which shroud the plants for days at a time. Succulent plants must be able to respond by absorbing the maximum amount of moisture in the shortest possible time.

To do this the plants have adopted a number of devices. Since small amounts of rain will not penetrate the soil to any great depth, the roots responsible for water acquisition lie close to the surface. In general, only those tall and heavy plants which need stabilising produce roots extending deep into the soil. The root systems of most succulent plants spread to a considerable distance from the plant body to gather moisture from a large catchment area.

Some succulent plants, in particular some of the columnar cacti of the mountains, have a covering of hair. This undoubtedly serves more than one purpose, but among these can be included the collection of moisture droplets from mist, which may then be absorbed into the body or allowed to fall to the ground for collection by the roots.

Having acquired water, the plant faces a battle with the elements to retain it. Desert temperatures tend to be high during the day and this, coupled with low humidity, provides ideal conditions for water loss by transpiration and evaporation. This would lead to desiccation and the eventual death of most plants, but succulents have developed a number of strategies to retain moisture. The most obvious is to modify the shape of the plant. A shape having a low ratio between surface area and volume is efficient in retaining water, the optimum being a sphere. Many succulent plants, in particular cacti, come close to this ideal. Some have truly spherical bodies while others have fattened stems producing a columnar shape. Other attempts at approaching the ideal shape are made by rosette plants which curl their leaves inwards during periods of drought. Other plants possess leaves which are fleshy and approach a spherical shape.

Fig 8 Echinocereus delaetii.

Fig 9 Mammillaria plumosa.

The second strategy is to store water in special cells. Cutting open a cactus stem or the fleshy leaf of a succulent reveals that the interior consists in the main of large water-storing cells. It has been estimated that the large 'organ pipe' cacti may contain thousands of litres of water, comprising over 90 per cent of the volume of the plant. This potential source of water has been the subject of numerous accounts of travellers lost in the desert being saved by slicing off the top of a cactus and drinking the contents.

A group of succulents and a small number of cacti store water in large tuberous roots which, being underground, are protected from the direct heat of the sun. These so-called caudiciform plants are enjoying a period of popularity with collectors, and are much sought after. In cultivation, where the compost is likely to be somewhat moister than the soil in habitat, they are usually grown with the tuber partly exposed.

All plants lose water by transpiration, a form of evaporation through pores (known as stomata) in the skin. Succulent plants have fewer stomata and these are located at the bottom of pits in the skin to reduce transpiration. In addition, some succulent plants have adopted an unusual form of photosynthesis known as Crassulacean Acid Metabolism (CAM), by which carbon dioxide is fixed during night-time rather than during the day. This process allows the plant to keep its stomata closed during the day-time heat. To reduce water loss further, many succulents have a waxy coating, sometimes appearing as a powdery bloom on the surface of the stem or leaves.

There are many other devices adopted by succulents to assist water conservation. A covering of hair or wool protects the plant body from the direct heat of the sun. Some succulents are deciduous and shed their leaves during periods of drought. In others which possess fleshy leaves, drought may cause the leaves to wither back from the tip, thus reducing the surface area and hence water loss. Fleshy-stemmed plants can survive extreme conditions of drought, which may cause a loss of up to two-thirds of their water content. They can do this by shrinking in diameter and also withdrawing into the soil. When rain falls again the plants absorb huge quantities and rapidly return to normal.

HISTORY OF DISCOVERY AND INTRODUCTION

Although there is little doubt that, from earliest times, the indigenous inhabitants have been aware of succulent plants growing in their localities, and have gathered and cultivated those considered useful, the association of Europeans with these plants dates from the latter part of the fifteenth century.

The first explorer of note was Columbus, who reached the West Indies in 1492. There his sailors would have seen a number of cacti and probably took a few back home as souvenirs. Certainly the plants are mentioned in documents written in Spain a few years later. It is possible that some of the 'prickly pears' now growing around the Mediterranean might be descendants of plants carried back on the *Santa Maria*. Within a few years the colonisation of North America began and more cacti and some of the other succulents were discovered.

In the early years of the sixteenth century the Spaniards Cortés and Pizarro conquered Mexico and a large part of South America to establish the colony of New Spain. Botanical exploration did not follow hard on the heels of military conquest however. Spain prevented foreigners from entering the colony, and it was not until the eighteenth century that botanists were able to investigate the flora.

Predating Columbus's landfall in the West Indies by a few years, the first contact with southern Africa by a European was made by the Portuguese sailor Dias. Within a few years European vessels were dropping anchor at the Cape of Good Hope to pick up water before continuing to the Far East. The first settlement was established by the Dutch in 1652 with the object of supplying the ships' crews. By the end of the century plants and seeds were being sent to Holland and from there found their way to botanical gardens in other countries. Among these were the first succulents from southern Africa.

By the beginning of the nineteenth century there were many large collections in private hands in Britain and elsewhere in Europe. This was a period when wealthy collectors vied to acquire rare specimens, and plants sometimes changed hands for more than their weight in gold. Nurseries specialising in cacti and succulents were established and some employed their own field collectors to gather plants from the wild. Then came a change in fashion; cacti and succulents were supplanted by orchids which required different growing conditions. The large succulent collections were discarded or declined, and interest in the plants waned until the turn of the present century when they were restored to favour. Their popularity has continued to the present time.

SUCCULENTS AS USEFUL PLANTS

As gardeners, we are attracted to cacti and succulents by their aesthetic qualities and do not consider their utilitarian value. For the indigenous people of the areas where the plants occur, who have a comparable struggle for survival, these plants have many useful applications.

Many plants have long been (and still are) used as a source of food. The most obvious use is for the fruit, and that of many species of *Opuntia* –

Fig 10 Rebutia ritteri

prickly pears – is gathered to be eaten raw or converted into jam. The larger seeds of some cacti and succulents are extracted and ground into meal as a source of starch. In southern Africa the fruits of *Carpobrotus edulis*, known as the 'Hottentot Fig', are eaten. The stems of various plants are also used as foodstuff. In Mexico the use of tender stems of cacti as a vegetable dates from thousands of years ago: the 'nopalitos' are still enjoyed today. The use of the central core of the agave is more destructive as collecting it entails cutting out the growing point. Another ancient use of the flesh of cacti that is still in vogue is the production of 'cactus candy'.

The ingenuity of the native peoples in using succulents as food was extended to produce a range of alcoholic drinks from fermented fruit juice or sap. The sap extracted from various species of *Agave* is still used to produce pulque and tequila. Other parts of the plants have also found their uses. Flowers are cooked as vegetables or used as a source of nectar. The large tuber of *Dioscorea elephantipes*, 'Hottentot Bread', is used for food in southern Africa.

Like most plant groups, succulents have found manifold applications in native medicine since ancient times. Sometimes the claims advanced for their efficacy appear exaggerated. For example, a sixth-century Greek herbal recommended one species of *Aloe* as a purgative, to heal wounds, treat boils, haemorrhoids, ulcers and headaches, induce sleep and prevent baldness. The ancients were probably wiser than credited, however, as the same plant is today used in the treatment of radiation burns. Another *Aloe* was hung in the hut of a barren woman to restore fertility. In contrast, a species of *Dioscorea* is today used in the manufacture of contraceptive pills. Another *Dioscorea* is used in the production of cortisone drugs.

More mundane uses have been found for inedible parts of the plants. Cactus spines have been used by the Indian peoples as needles, combs and fish-hooks. In the Galápagos Islands the cactus finch uses a cactus spine as a tool to extract grubs from crevices. The hair and wool of some cacti are sometimes used to stuff bedding. Fibres extracted from the leaves of various

Fig 11 Euphorbia echinus.

species of *Agave* have been used to make bowstrings and rope, and have been woven into coarse cloth. The species *Agave sisalina* is grown commercially for the production of sisal fibre.

Some succulents contain a poisonous sap. This has been used for the treatment of a variety of medical problems in both humans and animals, sometimes with fatal results. In both Africa and the Americas poisonous sap from succulent plants is used to tip hunting arrows. Other saps are used as a poison which is poured into a river to paralyse the fish without rendering them inedible. In Namibia the natives make use of *Sarcocaulon* plants, which contain a resin, as 'Bushman's candles'. The live plants can be burnt as torches. There have been attempts to use the latex produced by several species of *Euphorbia* to produce a kind of rubber, but the quality of the material is inferior to both natural and synthetic products.

The ancient Aztecs produced a red dye, not from a cactus but from the cochineal insect which fed on the plant. The Spanish conquerors brought insects back to Europe in the sixteenth century. Plantations of *Opuntia* were established, notably in the Canary Islands, and a thriving industry developed. In the latter part of the nineteenth century the Canary Islands exported some 2,500 tons of cochineal a year. The industry collapsed when aniline dyes were developed.

These are just a few of the multifarious uses to which succulents have been put, but they suffice to indicate that the plants have values other than their undoubted aesthetic ones.

CHAPTER 2

Cultivation

PROVIDING A SATISFACTORY ENVIRONMENT

Before plants are acquired, it is advisable to give attention to the conditions in which they will be grown. Although it might appear desirable to simulate the conditions occurring in the habitat, there is no way that this can be achieved. Even a small collection is likely to include plants from different parts of the world. Some may come from low altitudes where the seasonal variation in temperature is only a few degrees and rain falls in the winter. Others may come from high altitudes where temperatures range from high during the day to below freezing point at night and rain falls during the summer. Some plants may receive all their annual water supply during a period of a few weeks, followed by many months of drought when the plants shrink and withdraw into the soil. Others may be perpetually shrouded in mist and absorb most of their water intake through the skin rather than the roots.

Clearly it is not possible to provide conditions on a windowsill or in a greenhouse which parallel the conditions found in any one of these habitats. Instead, the collector should aim to provide conditions acceptable to the majority of the plants that will be grown, even though this will represent a compromise rather than an ideal state for any of them.

It is likely that the newcomer will start by growing plants in the home. It is possible to grow excellent specimens there, provided that due attention is paid to satisfying the basic requirements. The most important consideration must be the provision of adequate light. Apart from a handful of types, in particular the epiphytic plants, succulents are exposed to strong sunlight in the wild. In the home they must be positioned where they will receive the maximum amount of natural light. The ideal situation is a broad windowsill on the south side of the house, where they should be positioned not too close to the glass in order to avoid the possibility of scorching. Under no circumstances should plants be placed in dark corners or on top of the television set: though they may look very attractive initially, within a short time they will lose their colour, become etiolated and not flower.

The majority of succulent plants do not require high temperatures: all that is necessary is to maintain a temperature just above freezing point during the winter. A living-room windowsill, particularly if a radiator is positioned beneath it, may be too warm. The problem arises during the winter months. If the plants are kept dry, the high temperatures may cause them to shrivel excessively. If they are watered to maintain turgidity, they will continue to grow but the lower level of natural lighting will cause the plants to become misshapen. It would be better to move the plants to a cooler position, still with good lighting, for the winter.

The subject of composts is one which can be guaranteed to generate discussion among gardeners of all types. There is, however, nothing 'magic' about composts for succulents. All that is necessary is to provide a compost which drains freely, since stagnant moisture will kill succulents more rapidly than drought. The incorporation of coarse grit into proprietary loam-based or soil-less compost will provide the required drainage characteristics.

The final essential is to provide a suitable

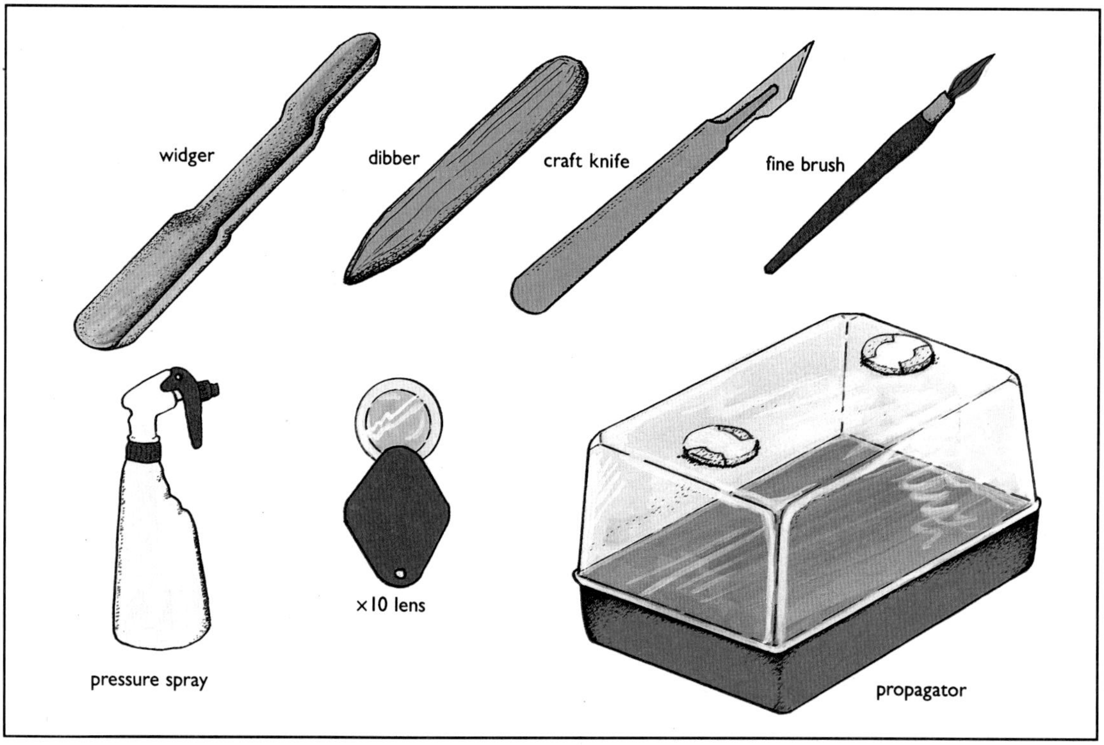

Fig 12 A range of useful implements for cultivating cacti and other succulents.

watering regime. The popular view of cacti as denizens of the desert sometimes leads to the plants being treated as inanimate objects and given no water at all. The net result is either that the plant slowly dies, or that the owner is enlightened, overwaters the plant in an excess of contrition and kills it more quickly. Ideally the plant should have water available to its roots all the time it is growing. For most this means that the compost should be just moist during the summer months and dry during the winter resting period. Care must be taken, though, as some succulents grow during the winter and rest during the summer. The best rule of thumb is to withhold water if the compost remains wet for any length of time after watering.

The conditions described above can be achieved on a windowsill and excellent free-flowering specimens can be grown there. A conservatory provides the possibility of growing larger plants and has the advantage that it is easier there to avoid extremes of temperature and to maintain a more buoyant atmosphere than in a living-room.

A greenhouse is the zenith of desirable residences for domesticated succulent plants. There they receive the maximum amount of light, the temperature can be controlled by heating in the winter and ventilation in the summer, and the plants can be provided with water and if necessary sprayed with chemicals without precipitating domestic disputes. It is important that the greenhouse should be positioned in an open situation where it will not be overshadowed by buildings or trees. It is simple to reduce the intensity of lighting by shading, but impossible to increase the intensity if it is insufficient.

Owners of small gardens which cannot accommodate a greenhouse should not overlook the possibilities afforded by a frame. These offer many of the benefits of a greenhouse and even have the advantage that the smaller volume is less expensive to heat. The range of plants that can be grown in a frame is limited to the shorter-growing types by the lack of headroom, though this can be increased by raising the frame on low walls.

Fig 13 A healthy collection of cacti and succulents on a windowsill.

PLANNING A COLLECTION

In the early stages of building a collection, it is desirable that a wide range of types is grown. This will provide invaluable experience in cultivation, and will also point the collector towards the plants which attract him or her most. If the environment in which the plants are grown is less than ideal, some kinds will grow more successfully than others. For example, if the only windowsill available for the plants faces north, it may be found that types which naturally occur in exposed positions where they are subjected to intense light will become etiolated. Others, occurring in shaded situations in the natural habitat, may grow and flower very well on the windowsill. This experience may encourage the collector to discard the former types and acquire more of the latter.

It is a fairly common experience, when stewarding an exhibition, to be approached by someone clutching a 'wants list' of plants who wishes to know where they may be obtained. Usually the names have been noted from illustrations in books, and unfortunately the illustrated plants, though appealing, are often quite unsuitable for a novice. They may be difficult to find, expensive to purchase, demanding to cultivate and quick to die. A few experiences of this kind may deter the novice who would have been equally happy and much more successful with different plants. The newcomer to the hobby is strongly advised to gain experience with easily obtained, inexpensive and undemanding plants.

As experience is gained, it may be found that interest in one group grows to the point where the collector begins to specialise. This specialisation may take various forms. Some growers concentrate on a single genus and attempt to 'collect the set'. This may lead to the collector contacting

Fig 14 There is an enormous range of succulent plants for the new collector to choose from.

other growers with a similar enthusiasm, studying the literature, making observations and eventually becoming something of an expert on that group of plants. Other growers may collect plants from a number of genera which grow in a particular area. This can be very interesting, as it reveals something of the relationships between plants responding to the same environmental conditions.

There are many other possibilities for specialised collecting. Cacti and succulents occasionally produce malformations in which the growing point ceases to produce symmetrical radial growth and instead develops into a growing line. The resultant growth, in the form of a convoluted fan or crest, is often very attractive. Other freak forms include variegated plants, which are also attractive enough to be brought together in a specialised collection.

It is advisable to build such thematic collections alongside a general collection, otherwise the scope for collecting is restricted. As collectors come into contact with other enthusiasts, they should not be seduced into following the latest fashion which could lead them to turn from the plants that really interest them to others of less appeal that happen, for the moment, to be in the limelight.

WHERE TO OBTAIN PLANTS

In order to build a collection, it is necessary to acquire plants. So where are they to be obtained? Plants may be acquired from a variety of sources, some more reliable than others.

First in line, in terms of both quantity and quality, are the specialist nurseries. In Britain there are a handful of commercial nurseries which have been supplying plants to collectors for many years. Their proprietors have an enthusiasm for succulents and a wealth of experience in their cultivation. They propagate thousands of plants every year and in some cases import more from specialist growers overseas to expand the range they offer. Generally they can be relied upon to offer clean, healthy, well-grown plants at reasonable prices, and to be willing to offer advice to novices. There are also many small nurseries, some of which operate on a part-time basis. Often these nurseries have been born out of the enthusiasm of their proprietors for propagation as a means of increasing their own collections. These nurseries are well worth visiting. Although they do not offer such a wide range as the larger nurseries, it is often possible to find uncommon plants that are not available elsewhere.

Fig 15 A specialist nursery is the best place to buy plants when starting a new collection.

The larger garden centres deal in a very wide range of plants and many of them offer succulents. These are usually grown by specialists, often overseas, and tend to be the more easily grown types. Where turnover of stock is high, the frequently changing display offers the opportunity of acquiring a variety of plants. The labelling of succulent plants in a garden centre can cause problems. Often only a generic name appears on the label, while a few give the plants 'popular' names. This need not discourage purchasers: the plants are usually clean and healthy and identifying them is not too difficult.

Florists' shops and chainstores are less reliable sources. The plants offered are obtained from a variety of suppliers and vary considerably in

Fig 16 Crassula barklyi.

quality. They should not be totally disregarded though: it is possible to find bargains and superb show-winning specimens have been grown from tiny seedlings acquired from chainstores.

Specialist societies are a fruitful source of inexpensive plants. The societies hold frequent meetings where surplus plants may be offered at low prices, and among these many bargains can be found. Look out for advertisements for the specialist shows, usually held in early summer. By visiting them, the novice can see a wide range of superbly grown specimen plants and may be able to purchase smaller examples from the sales stands.

SELECTING SUITABLE PLANTS

To select plants that will provide satisfaction, it is desirable that the grower should have some knowledge of the basic characteristics of the most frequently encountered types. If the collection is to be grown on a windowsill, the types which grow rapidly to a large size should be avoided and the smaller growing types sought. Such knowledge is acquired slowly, but by visiting shows, studying displays and, best of all, talking with other enthusiasts, the novice will develop a 'feel' for the plants most suitable for his or her own environment. In particular, by visiting nurseries and shows during the early summer, when many of the plants are likely to be in flower, the novice will be able to see which types flower at a small size.

Having located a plant which has aesthetic appeal and which appears suitable for the available conditions, how can the novice check its health? The first inspection should be of the container and compost, since these can provide an indication of potential problems. A plant that is loose in its compost may have lost its roots. Soggy compost hints at incipient rot which begins at the roots and spreads rapidly up through the plant body, only becoming apparent to the casual eye when too late to remedy. Purchasers should also be on their guard if the compost is compacted. Occasionally plants are offered in strange composts which set like concrete. Although they may survive in such material, problems can arise when the plants are transferred to a different compost. Ideally, the plant should be firmly potted in a compost that is friable and just moist.

Assuming that all is well with the compost, attention can be turned to the plant itself. A healthy plant should be turgid but not bloated. A plant that looks about to burst has probably been over-fed and over-watered. Such growth is tender and susceptible to damage. Returning the plant to a correct growing regime usually causes a change in characteristics such as body diameter, density of spination or leaf size produced thereafter, which spoils the appearance of the plant. At the other extreme, the plant should not be desiccated. If it is badly shrivelled, this suggests that the plant has been left dry for too long or that the roots are damaged and incapable of taking up moisture.

Consideration should be given to the shape and colour of the plant. If it has been kept for too long in poor light it may be etiolated, with the youngest growth paler in colour than the remainder. Etiolation, unless extreme, is unlikely to kill the plant, but the distortion of growth is permanent and the plant will always appear misshapen.

The plant should be carefully inspected for indications of disease or pest infestation. Brown, black or orange marks on the body, particularly at soil level, suggest that the plant is suffering from a fungal attack which is likely to be fatal. If the region of the growing point is pale brown, the plant probably has red spider mite. The larger pests such as mealy bugs should be easily seen. Never purchase such plants: even though it

Fig 17 × Chamaelobivia *'Purple Bess'*.

may be possible to cure the complaint, it is more likely that it will spread to the rest of your collection.

Never purchase succulent plants that are offered for sale outside florists' shops during the winter. Pavement displays of such plants as the popular Christmas Cactus are colourful and attractive, but plants that have been exposed to the icy blast of a British winter are likely to show the effects some time later.

Finally, do not be tempted by the so-called 'flowering cacti' offered by some unscrupulous dealers. These monstrosities are produced by attaching plastic or 'everlasting' flowers to seedling cacti, usually by sticking the 'flower' stalks into the plant body. Apart from being aesthetically displeasing (to the true cactophile), such plants are likely to succumb within a short time to fungus entering the wounds. Better to buy a plastic cactus which at least has the merit of not necessitating the death of a living plant.

CONSERVATION AND IMPORTATION

In recent years there has been a growing recognition that the flora and fauna of our world are under threat from a variety of agencies, which have caused the disappearance of some and brought others to the brink of extinction. Although succulent plants lack the public appeal of the giant panda, some species are nevertheless in similar danger. Fortunately, many countries have enacted legislation to protect not only their own flora but also that of other countries. This legislation takes the form of restrictions on collecting plants from the wild (or even picking their flowers) and on the importation of both wild-collected and nursery-propagated plants.

In the United Kingdom, regulations are based on the recommendations made by the Convention on International Trade in Endangered Species (CITES), enforced by the Department of the Environment. So far as it affects succulents, the importation of an extensive list of wild-collected species is totally banned. The importation of an even more extensive list of nursery-propagated succulents (including all cacti) requires the importer to obtain a licence from the D.o.E. HM Customs are empowered to seize plants not accompanied by the appropriate licence, while those attempting to import them are liable to prosecution.

The sensible approach is to avoid trouble. When visiting countries where succulent plants are endemic, resist the temptation to dig them up. An appealing cactus is not worth the risk of a spell in a foreign gaol. If planning to visit nurseries on the Continent with the intention of purchasing succulents, obtain the necessary licence from the D.o.E. well in advance and familiarise yourself with the plants that you are not permitted to import. It should be recognised that some nurseries on the Continent offer for sale plants that cannot be imported into the UK.

CONTAINERS

When plants are cultivated indoors, they are usually planted in containers. In larger greenhouses and conservatories there may be sufficient space to accommodate a semi-natural plant bed, which can be attractive but suffers from several disadvantages. The most immediately apparent problem is that the free root-run encourages some plants to make rapid growth. In no time the taller growing plants are threatening to go through the roof, while the shrubby types expand beyond their allotted space to smother their weaker brethren. Watering is difficult to regulate and pest control also becomes a problem. An infestation of soil-borne pests may be impossible to eradicate without dismantling the bed and replacing all the compost. Containers usually provide a better environment for succulents.

By and large, succulents are not fussy about the containers in which they are grown. They can be cultivated quite successfully in plastic pots, earthenware (clay) pots, concrete troughs, wooden

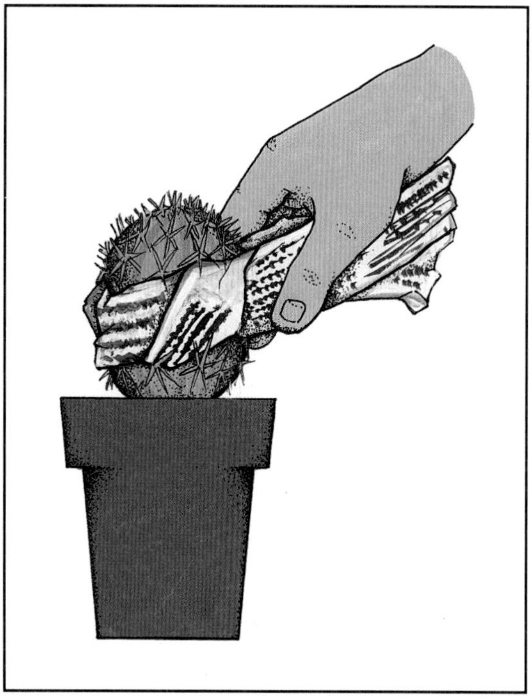

Fig 18 A helpful method of handling spiny plants.

Fig 19 Senecio haworthii.

boxes, metal cans, glass jars or discarded yoghurt containers. However, all but the first two have disadvantages. To grow plants in containers without drainage holes requires some skill, otherwise the compost becomes waterlogged and the plants rot. Metal cans tend to corrode and wooden boxes to decay. Perhaps the most important aspect is their lack of aesthetic appeal. Discarded yoghurt pots may be useful as a temporary abode for a rooting cutting, but usually the choice lies between plastic and clay pots.

The major difference between these hinges on their water-retaining qualities. The wall of a clay pot is porous, allowing water to pass through. In consequence, moisture is drawn from the compost and is evaporated at the outer surface. The compost in a small pot dries out rapidly, so it is necessary to water more frequently. Conversely, the compost is less likely to become waterlogged. The process of evaporation from the outer surface cools the pot, preventing the roots from being cooked during sunny weather. The wall of a plastic pot is impervious, so the compost remains moist for a longer period. This can be a disadvantage with larger pots, which may remain moist all through the winter.

By adjusting the proportion of drainage material incorporated into the compost, it is possible to balance the water-retaining properties of the two types of container. It is then feasible to mix the two, using small plastic pots for those plants that require a reasonable amount of water and small clay pots for those that are more sensitive. For the larger plants, clay pots have advantages: they do not retain so much moisture during the winter, and their greater weight helps to provide stability. Against this, a large plant in a clay pot is difficult to lift.

COMPOSTS

There are probably more compost recipes than growers of succulents. Most collectors have a favourite mixture; some have several for different groups of succulents. One book published some years ago listed no less than twenty-five different mixtures for a single genus. This is bewildering for the novice looking for a simple recipe that can be used for all the plants. He or she sees beautifully grown specimens and is told that they are grown in such-and-such compost, then another group of equally wonderful plants that are grown in a totally different compost. How does the novice make sense of this conflict?

It must be realised that the compost has to fulfil several functions. First it must provide an anchorage for the roots. By their nature, tall-growing succulents tend to be top-heavy. The compost must provide stability to prevent them from falling over. This is accomplished by having a mixture of particle sizes, from small pebbles and rock chips down to sand grains, which interlock and prevent excessive movement when the compost is watered.

The compost must also have the ability to retain water for long enough for the roots to absorb it. This function is satisfied by humus in the compost, which may be in the form of peat, leaf-mould or other organic material. Alternatively, there are a number of inert, inorganic materials, such as perlite and vermiculite, which can absorb and retain large quantities of water.

It is not a contradiction that the compost must also be free-draining. Ideally, when the compost is watered the bulk of the water should pass through quickly, leaving the compost just moist but with the water-retaining material acting like tiny sponges and holding water for a longer period. To improve the drainage properties, material such as grit or coarse sand may be incorporated.

The compost must contain the nutrients necessary for growth. The most important of these are nitrogen, phosphorus and potassium, but there are several others, known as trace elements, that are required in minute quantities. The nutrients must be in a form in which they can be absorbed by the roots, and since these can only absorb liquids the nutrients must be in solution. Normally the nutrients are incorporated into the compost in powder form and are made

Fig 20 Echinocereus knippelianus.

available to the roots when the plant is watered.

With this understanding, it is now possible to consider the alternatives. There are two basic types: those based on loam and those based on peat. The proprietary loam-based types are usually offered as John Innes composts and are mixed in accordance with the formula developed at the John Innes Horticultural Institute. This is a simple one, comprising seven parts (by volume) of sterilised loam, three parts of horticultural peat and two parts of coarse sand. To this should be added base fertiliser in the proportion of 1oz (25g) to a standard (2 gallon) bucket of compost. The loam is a critical component and proprietary mixtures vary considerably. Those growers who prefer to mix their own compost should note that ordinary garden soil is rarely suitable, unless taken from well-cultivated land into which humus has been incorporated over a long period.

There are several proprietary peat-based composts, produced by mixing a drainage material with sphagnum or sedge peat and adding a fertiliser. As peat is usually more consistent than loam, hobbyists can mix their own compost with reasonable confidence. The usual ratio is three parts (by volume) of peat to one of coarse sand, grit or perlite. Several horticultural suppliers offer a suitable base fertiliser in convenient sachets.

Both types of compost are likely to require the addition of material to increase their free-draining properties. The amount required is best determined by experiment as it will depend on the initial constituents of the compost, but as a rough guide one part of grit or perlite added to three parts of compost should be satisfactory.

What are the relative merits of the two basic types of compost? The peat-based composts are usually more consistent than the loam-based types. They are lighter, so handling large plants is easier. They tend to retain moisture for a longer period, so require less frequent watering. Against this can be set the fact that they are more difficult to moisten once allowed to dry out. Nutrients are more quickly leached out, so supplementary feeding or more frequent repotting is necessary. In an attempt to obtain the best features of both types, some suppliers offer a universal compost which is a combination of the two.

It would be inadvisable to recommend a particular compost for all growers. Some growers will have greater success with one type, others with a different one. Fortunately, succulent plants are tolerant of a wide variety of composts and the novice should experiment, note which variant suits his or her conditions best, then stick with it. Switching frequently from one compost to another in an attempt to obtain results similar to those achieved by other growers is rarely successful.

POTTING AND REPOTTING

Cacti and succulents are usually acquired as young plants in small pots. Within a short period the faster-growing types will need to be repotted. The prospect often fills the novice with trepidation. There is no reason for panic however: provided reasonable care is taken, the plant can be transferred safely and will grow on without a check.

The first requirement is to select a suitable container. Pots are available in a range of sizes and shapes, and consideration should be given to choosing one to complement the plant. Usually the new pot will need to be a little larger than the original, though slow-growing plants may be repotted into the same size, merely replacing the exhausted compost with fresh material. Generally the plant should look 'balanced' and in harmony with its pot. For globular plants a pot slightly larger than the plant's diameter is suitable. Columnar and shrubby plants will need a larger pot to provide accommodation for their generally sturdier root systems and to maintain stability. The depth of the pot should be selected to match the plant's root system. Plants with a sparse root system may grow better in shallow half-pots or pans, while those with long, stout roots may be better in 'long tom' pots. Some plants have a massive, tuberous root and a small body. These are usually better in pots only slightly larger than the tuberous root. Never put a plant into a pot that is much too large in the hope that this will encourage it to grow more rapidly. Usually the reverse affect will be obtained: the compost remains wet and the plant's rate of growth slows even if the root does not rot.

The plant should be watered the day before it is to be repotted, so that the compost is moist but not wet. This will make removal of the old pot easier. The fresh compost should also be uniformly moist. A handful picked up and gently squeezed should cling together, but should crumble apart when dropped back on to the heap.

To remove a small plant from its pot, place a hand over the compost, arranging the fingers around the base of the plant if possible. If the size or shape of the plant body prevents this, place the hand on top of the plant or around the stem. Heavily spined cacti can be a problem, but a thick layer of rags or pieces of expanded polystyrene will protect the hand and the plant. Inverting the plant and pot may cause the root-ball

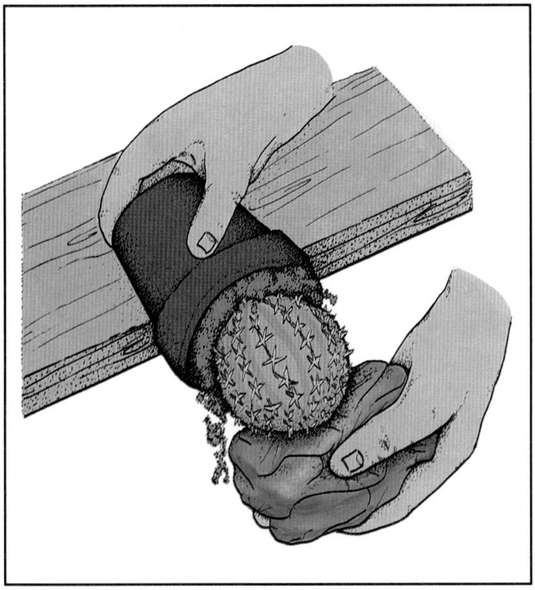

Fig 21 A painless method of removing a cactus from a pot.

to slide out of the pot under its own weight. If not, a plastic pot can be gently squeezed out of shape to free the plant. Plants in clay pots can be more obstinate, but giving the edge of the pot a sharp tap on the bench will usually do the trick. If all else fails, it may be necessary to break the pot. Removing a large plant from its pot can be more difficult. It may be safer to place the pot on its side and give the rim and base a few sharp blows to loosen the root-ball.

Once the root-ball is accessible it is possible gently to tease much of the old compost away from the roots. If the plant has been in the same pot for several years, the root-ball may contain very little of the original compost. It is desirable to remove as much as possible of the exhausted compost, but care should be taken to avoid damaging the roots. At the same time the roots should be carefully inspected for evidence of root mealy bug (*see* Chapter 3).

The new pot is prepared by placing a small quantity of drainage material in the form of coarse peat, small pebbles, chippings or dried leaves in the bottom. If the drainage holes are large it may be necessary to cover them first with something that will retain the finer compost but allow surplus water to escape. Small pieces of perforated zinc sheet, plastic netting or discarded nylon stockings can be used, but avoid anything that will rot. Place a small quantity of compost on top of this drainage layer. It may be advantageous to add a few granules of a soil pesticide at the same time. These will slowly evaporate over a period of time, producing a gas which permeates the compost to kill any insect pests.

The plant is then suspended such that when the container is filled the new compost will be at the same level on the plant body as was the original. It is very important that the plant body is not buried too deeply, which may induce rot, and that the roots are not left partly exposed. Fresh compost can now be trickled around the plant, taking care that the roots are not forced into a bunch in the centre of the pot but remain spread out. When the pot is full, the compost can be firmed gently with the fingers or by tapping the pot on the bench. The compost must not be compacted as this will damage the roots.

It is better not to water the plant for a week or so after repotting to allow time for any damage to heal and new roots to begin to form. If the weather is particularly warm, it may be advantageous to spray the plant body to prevent desiccation.

Repotting can be carried out at any time of year, but it is best done at the start of the growing season. This gives the plant the best possible chance of re-establishing itself quickly and growing away without a check. Plants repotted during their resting period should be left without water until they begin to show signs of fresh growth.

TEMPERATURE

The newcomer to the cultivation of succulent plants, observing their exotic appearance and learning that many are denizens of those parts of the world enjoying a warm climate, might be

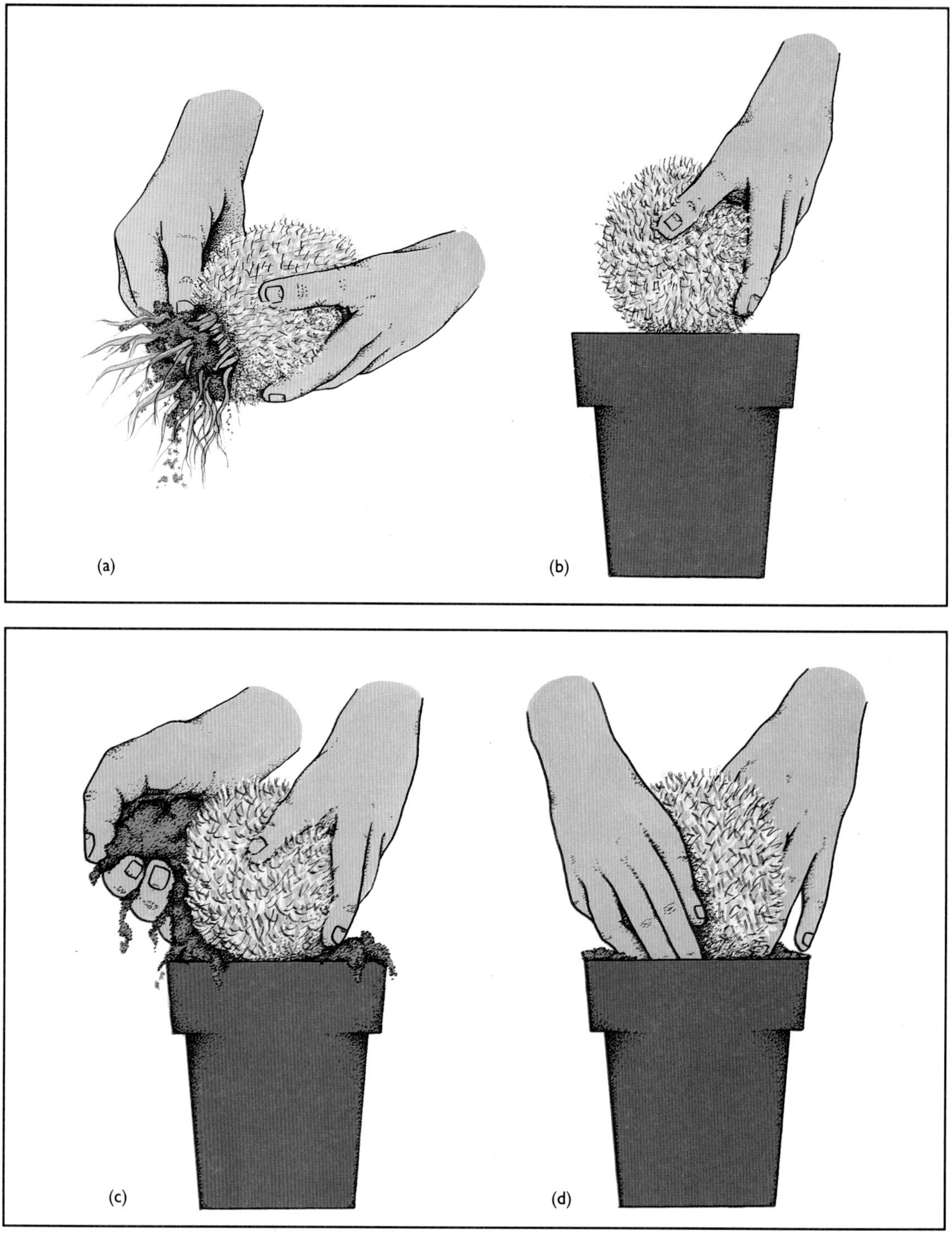

Fig 22 Potting; (a) remove the old compost from the roots of the cactus (b) place it carefully in a pot partially filled with fresh compost (c) finish filling the pot, working carefully around the cactus (d) gently firm it down, paying attention to the position of the cactus and its roots.

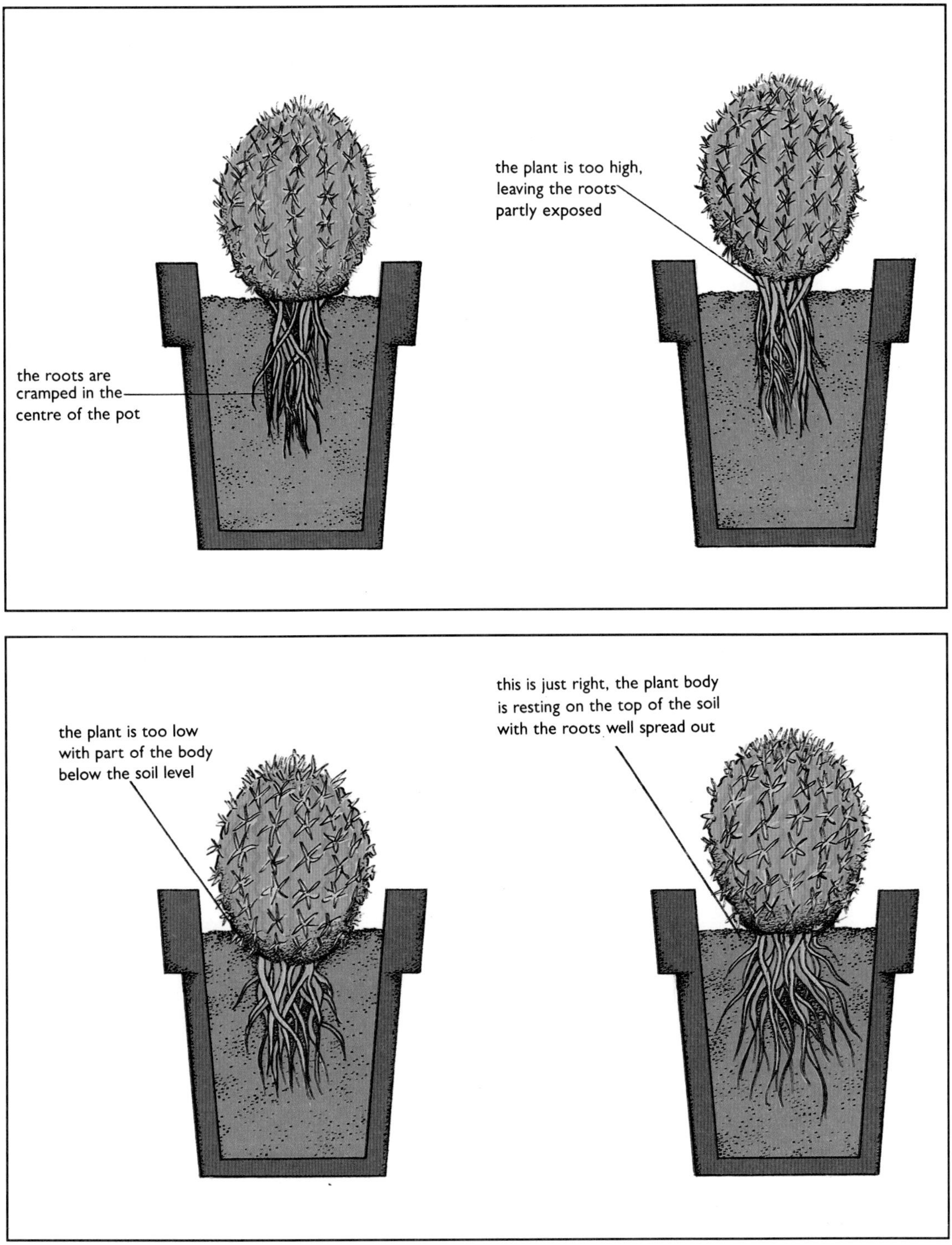

Fig 23 Here are some of the mistakes that can be made when potting up a cactus. The first three illustrations show how not to do it and the final illustration shows the correct position.

discouraged by consideration of the expense of providing a temperature to keep the plants happy during a British winter. However, novices will be reassured to learn that the majority of succulents are quite tolerant and can be grown successfully in an environment where the temperature falls close to freezing point.

There are a few plants which demand higher temperatures. In the main the cacti are restricted to a few genera, for example *Melocactus* and *Discocactus*, a few of the columnar plants from Brazil and some epiphytes. The more tender of the other succulents include some from the hot tropical regions of the Old World, from Madagascar, the Horn of Africa, the Arabian sub-continent and India. Not all of the succulents from these areas are tender though: some are content with conditions similar to those provided for the cacti. The novice is advised to forgo the pleasure of growing the more tender plants until experience has been gained – there is a sufficiency of attractive, free-flowering types that are less demanding.

Compared with conditions in Europe, the climate of the regions where many succulents grow exhibits, so far as temperature is concerned, a number of important differences. First, the annual mean temperatures are higher. Secondly, there are significant differences between the daily mean temperatures during the 'active' season when the plants are growing and the 'dormant' season when the plants rest. Thirdly, there are often great variations between the day-time temperature, which might reach 100 °F (40 °C), and the overnight temperature which may plummet to freezing point.

In cultivation, the temperature range within which the majority of succulents will be happy is a wide one. The important requirement is that high temperatures are associated with the

Fig 24 Mammillaria carmenae.

period of growth and low temperatures with the rest period. It is convenient that our warm season coincides with the growing season for most of the plants. There are a few, including the succulent species of *Pelargonium* and *Tylecodon*, that maintain the growth pattern appropriate to their southern hemisphere habitat, and insist on growing during our winter. These need a somewhat different treatment.

For the part of the year when there is no possibility of frost, there is no necessity for supplementary heating of a succulent plant collection. Natural solar heating will maintain a sufficiently high temperature for growth to take place. During this period, adequate ventilation is a more important requirement, to prevent overheating and to reduce the possibility of scorch damage. One might even leave greenhouse ventilators open day and night for much of this period.

Fig 25 Pachyphytum oviferum.

The winter, with its attendant low temperatures and high humidity, is the period when most cacti and succulents are dormant. While the plants should be protected from frost, there is no need to maintain a high temperature. On the contrary, a high temperature will encourage the plants to remain in growth, but the low intensity of natural light will tend to produce etiolation, spoiling the shape of the plants. It will also affect their flowering performance in the following season. The plants need a period at low temperature to prepare themselves for successful flowering. All that is required is to maintain a temperature a little above freezing point: 40–45 °F (5–7 °C) is ideal. If the plants are dormant and have been prepared for the winter by reducing the frequency of watering sufficiently early to allow the compost to dry out, most plants will come to no harm even if the temperature drops to just below freezing point for a few hours. Even at these low temperatures, ventilation is important. Every opportunity should be taken to open ventilators on sunny days, closing them well before sunset to allow the temperature to build up for the night.

While the conditions described above will satisfy the majority of the plants, there are still those that are a little more tender or which are in active growth during the winter period. How should they be treated? No matter how efficient the heating system, there will be a variation in temperature from place to place within a greenhouse. It is time well spent to investigate with a thermometer, locating the warmer and cooler areas. It is then possible to site the more tender plants in the warmer positions. The plants that are in active growth during the winter should be placed in a well-lit position. As they will need to be watered, it is as well to keep them warm too. It may be feasible to have a small area of the greenhouse at a higher temperature than the rest by adding local heating.

A word of warning for those collectors growing plants on a windowsill: the temperature of a heated living-room in winter is probably too high for the plants. They will continue growing, even if kept dry, and their flowering performance will suffer. It would be advantageous to move them to a cooler location for the winter months. Of course, they should still be provided with the best possible light.

HEATING METHODS

There are several alternative forms of heating, and the choice will depend on capital and running costs, availability of mains services and convenience.

The cheapest in terms of capital cost is likely to be a paraffin heater. These vary in size and hence output, so it is possible to use one or several to maintain the required temperature. Paraffin heaters suffer from a number of disadvantages compared with other heating methods. They are not suitable for thermostatic control, and the grower has to keep a close watch on weather forecasts and other indications in order to ensure that the heater is brought into use when frost is expected. The heaters need regular and careful maintenance: if they are allowed to smoke they will cover the plants with soot overnight. Not least is the disadvantage that the combustion process produces a large quantity of water vapour as a by-product, leading to an increase in humidity and the danger of moulds appearing and spreading through a greenhouse. That said, it may be that the siting of the greenhouse and the absence of other services precludes the use of an alternative, and many growers cope perfectly well with the shortcomings of the paraffin heater.

Gas, either from a main or from a cylinder, is another possibility. This too involves a combustion process and the production of water vapour, but it has the advantage that thermostatic control is possible. Some growers report adverse reactions by some of the leaf succulents, manifested as yellowing of the leaves, but this may also occur with paraffin heating. Gas heating tends to be more expensive to install than paraffin heating, but there are savings on running costs due to the use of thermostatic control.

Fig 26 Piaranthus decorus.

Electric heating has many advantages. It is clean, easily controlled and flexible. Tubular heaters, comprising an element contained within a tube, can be positioned beneath the staging so that warmth rises from beneath the plants. When running, the tubes become quite hot, so it is essential to ensure that plant stems and foliage do not touch them. Other variants have the element enclosed in an oil or water bath to produce a buffering effect and to allow for less frequent switching.

Fan heaters, in which air is blown through a heating element, are very effective in a greenhouse. In some types the fan runs continuously with the thermostatically controlled element switching on at intervals. This produces a more uniform distribution of heat, and in the summer improves the air circulation. Fan heaters are convenient, requiring a minimum of attention, but should not be treated casually. If an element fails, the fan will blow cold air over the plants, while if the thermostat fails the temperature may rise to unacceptable levels.

Soil-heating cables comprise a sheathed heating element which is buried in sand. They run at a fairly low temperature, so providing a gentle heat at all times, abrupt changes being avoided by the buffering action of the sand. Soil cables provide a useful way of generating local heat, since the heat lost contributes to the general heating of the whole area.

All forms of electric heating in a greenhouse are potentially lethal. Electricity and water do not mix! It is absolutely essential that power supplies to a greenhouse or frame are installed by a competent electrician and are provided with safety cut-outs.

WATERING

There is a popular misconception that succulent plants are somehow able to survive without water. While it is true that they are adapted to gather the meagre quantity available in an arid climate, and then to retain it through long periods of drought, like all plants they need a supply of water for survival.

The function of the water is to dissolve nutrients present in the soil so that they can be absorbed by the roots. The plant is only able to make use of nutrients in soluble form. Once absorbed, the nutrients are transported through the plant in its sap, the flow of which requires an intake of water at the roots and a loss by evaporation through the stomata in the skin and leaves.

In the habitat, soil moisture may be gathered by an extensive system of roots extending to a considerable distance from the plant stem, but in cultivation the plants are dependent on the watering-can wielded by their owner. The skill of the cultivator lies in providing sufficient water to satisfy the plants' needs, without making the compost so wet that the roots rot.

There is no simple recipe for success in watering. Recommendations such as 'once a week in summer, none in winter' are over-simplifications. Some of the water supplied will drain through the compost and out through the holes in the base of the pot. The fraction retained will depend on the structure of the compost: how much water-retaining material has been incorporated into it. Some of the retained water will be lost by evaporation from the surface, and through the container walls if they are porous. The rate of evaporation will be governed by the ambient temperature and humidity. The quantity of water taken up by the plant will depend on its size, its degree of succulence and its state of growth.

From this it follows that the grower must eschew the simple 'rule of thumb' and must instead apply intelligence to determine when to water. Plants in growth, particularly in small pots, are likely to need frequent and copious watering. Mature plants in large pots will require less frequent attention, as will highly succulent and slow-growing types. The plants should always be given sufficient water to ensure that the whole of the compost is moistened without becoming waterlogged. They should then be left until the

Fig 27 Lithops verruculosa v. glabra.

compost has begun to dry out before being watered again. If in doubt about whether or not to water, it is better to err on the side of caution. Under-watering will do less harm than over-watering. During the growing season the compost should not be allowed to dry out completely; if this happens it will cause a check in the growth of the plant.

Ideally, the plants should be watered by standing the pots in a shallow tray containing water to about a quarter of the depth of the pots. Capillary action will draw water up through the compost until the surface is damp. This method ensures that the whole of the root-ball is moistened. Unfortunately, this method is too time-consuming in the case of large collections, and the owner must resort to overhead watering from a can. The best time of day for overhead watering is early morning or late evening, which allows surplus water to evaporate from the plant bodies before they are exposed to bright sunlight. Care should always be taken not to leave globules of water on the plants: they act as small lenses when struck by the sun's rays, causing scorch marks on the plant.

Most succulents appreciate an occasional spraying with clean water. This helps to remove dust, and leaves the plant looking fresher. Note, however, that spraying may mark the powdery bloom on some plants.

The quality of the water used is often outside the control of the grower. Ideally, it should be neutral to slightly acid, and soft to slightly hard. Usually rainwater comes close to this ideal, except perhaps in industrial areas where it may be too acid or contain harmful substances washed out of the atmosphere, but it is rarely possible to collect and store sufficient rainwater to last through the year. Tapwater is often the only feasible alternative.

The level of acidity of the compost is important for optimal growth, and is affected by the acidity of the water used for watering. Acidity is described in terms of pH value on a scale 0–14. Pure water is neutral, with a value of pH 7.0. Values less than 7.0 indicate acidity, while values above 7.0 indicate alkalinity. The optimum range of values for the growth of most cacti and succulents is pH 6.0–7.0. Watering with alkaline water will gradually make the compost alkaline. Yellowing of foliage and skin (chlorosis) is often an indication that the compost is too alkaline.

Water hardness may be another problem. In some areas the mains water supply is hard, containing dissolved mineral salts. These modify the acidity of the compost, making it more alkaline, and also leave a whitish deposit at the base of the plant stem.

Acidity levels of compost and water supply can be checked quite easily by the grower, using a

Fig 28 Sulcorebutia zavaletae.

simple chemical indicator. If it is found desirable to increase the acidity of the water, this may be done by steeping a few handfuls of acid peat in it, or by carefully adding a few drops of nitric acid until the required level is reached.

FEEDING

The nutrients required by a growing plant fall into two categories. The basic elements nitrogen, phosphorus and potassium are required in relatively large amounts, while other elements, termed trace elements, are required in extremely minute quantities. The proportions of the basic elements required varies from one type of plant to another and from one part of the growing season to another.

Proprietary potting composts normally contain the required nutrients, as do those mixed by the grower in accordance with the recommendations made earlier. However, over a period of time the nutrients are gradually leached out as a consequence of watering and the compost becomes infertile. In the case of no-soil composts, this process may take only a few months. Cacti and succulents, when mature, may be repotted only annually or even less frequently, and to maintain them in good condition it is necessary to feed the plants with a suitable fertiliser. An understanding of the function of the main nutrients will help the grower to select a suitable type.

Nitrogen is responsible for building plant tissues such as stem and leaves. It is usually provided in the form of nitrates and ammonium compounds. Phosphorus, in the form of phosphate (superphosphate), encourages the production of flowers and the subsequent development of fruit and seeds. It also promotes the growth of a healthy and vigorous root system. Potassium increases the plants' resistance to disease. It is normally provided as potash. There are many fertilisers in which these elements are combined in different proportions, indicated by the NPK coding. For example, the coding 6–10–14

Fig 29 Huernia stapelioides.

Fig 30 Lobivia hertrichiana.

indicates a fertiliser containing a mixture of six parts of nitrogen, ten of phosphate and fourteen of potash.

At the beginning of the growing season, feeding with a high-nitrogen fertiliser gives the plants a good start, but continuing to use this fertiliser through the season will not suit the majority of succulent plants, as it will promote 'soft' growth that is susceptible to disease. Only in those cases where vigorous vegetative growth is desired, such as leaf succulents or those plants producing annual foliage from a storage organ – the so-called caudiciform plants – should use of this fertiliser be continued. For the majority of succulent plants it will be advantageous to change to a fertiliser containing a smaller proportion of nitrogen.

The essential trace elements include magnesium, iron, manganese, copper, zinc, boron and molybdenum. For satisfactory growth these are required in minute quantities, perhaps one part in ten million. This may seem an insignificant amount, but trace element deficiencies are accompanied by very visible symptoms, including chlorosis, distortion of the body and browning of the epidermis. Overdosing with trace elements to correct a real or imagined deficiency is dangerous as higher concentrations may poison the plant. Some proprietary fertilisers contain trace elements, and it is recommended that these be used.

Fertilisers are available both as powders to be mixed with the potting compost and as powders or liquids to be dissolved in water. When using liquid fertilisers, care should be taken not to splash the plant body, where evaporation may leave unsightly marks. Since most succulents are slow-growing, their nutritional requirements are less than those of many other plants, and it is recommended that the liquid feed is diluted to about half the normal strength. In order to avoid irregular growth, frequent watering with diluted fertiliser is better than less frequent applications of the standard strength.

DISPLAYING A COLLECTION

There is a world of difference between an accumulation of potted plants and an attractively displayed collection. No matter how perfectly grown the plants, if they are merely placed haphazardly in a group they will not command attention. Giving some thought to the individual specimens by planting them in appropriate containers, neatly labelling them and then arranging them in an attractive manner produces a display that will be pleasing to the owner and to visitors.

The choice of container has already been discussed from the practical aspect of cultivation. Consideration should also be given to aesthetics. The traditional clay and plastic pots are available in a wide range of sizes and shapes, and it is usually possible to select one to harmonise with the plant. Very large plants often pose a problem. The largest clay pots are exorbitantly expensive and large plastic pots are difficult to obtain, so the owner may be tempted to press into service such containers as plastic buckets and washing-up bowls. While these usually prove perfectly satisfactory for cultivation, they do nothing to enhance the appearance of the plants. It is better to seek out the containers sold for growing shrubs or decorating patios.

The colour of the containers is a matter of individual preference. Terracotta-coloured clay pots have been with us for long enough to be universally accepted. Plastic pots are available in a variety of colours, among which terracotta, black and dark green are the most pleasing. Some of the other colours available – bright red, yellow and pale blue – are less harmonious and a mixture of these produces a clash of colour that offends the eye!

In order to communicate with other enthusiasts, a knowledge of plant names is indispensable to the grower. Rather than rely on memory, most prefer to label their plants. If neat labels are used in an unobtrusive way, they will not detract from the appearance of the collection. Plastic labels are available in a range of shapes (straight and tee) and sizes. Most can be

Fig 31 Stapelia semota.

written on using waterproof ink, some will accept pencil and others are inscribed by means of a special tool. They are generally long-lasting, though some inks fade in sunlight and most eventually become brittle and will have to be replaced. Wooden labels eventually rot.

The collection may be arranged in various ways, at the discretion of the grower. Some may prefer to group related plants together in order to study taxonomic aspects. Others may take advantage of the temperature variation throughout a greenhouse to bring together those plants requiring similar treatment. Probably the majority will simply aim to display the plants attractively. There is a sufficient variety of shape and colour among succulent plants to appeal to the artistic instinct. Generally speaking, the taller plants should be positioned at the back of the display and the smaller ones at the front, but a row of similar columnar plants at the back and serried ranks of smaller ones at the front is not particularly appealing.

For those with sufficient space, there is the possibility of arranging plants in a bed. By incorporating a few pieces of natural rock – not lumps of concrete – it is possible to create a display that looks quite natural. The long-term problems associated with growing plants in beds have been discussed, but there is an alternative: the temporary outdoor bed. Most succulents benefit from a sojourn in the open during the summer, and a display bed is more attractive than rows of pots. The most suitable site is one that will receive as much direct sun as possible. The plants may be left in their pots, which should be plunged to the rim and disguised by a few pieces of rock or a layer of chippings. This has two advantages: the plants do not grow too vigorously, and it is an easy matter to lift them for return to the greenhouse. Outdoors the plants will be at the mercy of the mollusc population, so protective measures are essential.

Fig 32 Neohenricia sibbettii.

GENERAL ADVICE

The cultural advice offered here should not be regarded as an infallible recipe for success. A regime that is completely satisfactory for one grower may prove to be a failure with another. The important thing is to experiment, observe effects, adopt successful methods and learn from mistakes. If a plant seems to be ailing, is not growing or refuses to flower, do not jump to conclusions. Try moving it to a different position where it will receive more light or will be warmer. Examine the compost and modify the watering regime. If all this fails, remove the plant from the compost and check the condition of the roots. Check the acidity of the compost and water you are using. Try a different fertiliser. If any of these actions results in improvement, take note but do not necessarily treat all the other plants in the collection in the same way. If the others are thriving, let well alone.

Pay particular attention to hygiene in the greenhouse. Do not leave dead plants among healthy ones, encouraging disease or pests to spread. Remove dead leaves, flower remains and over-ripe fruits; they are potential sources of disease and hiding places for pests. A few minutes spent every week on the removal of such material may avoid the heartache of losing a cherished plant.

CHAPTER 3

Pests, Diseases and Other Problems

PESTS

Someone once defined a weed as a plant in the wrong place. Similarly, while there are creatures that are intentionally destructive of succulents, there are others that are merely a nuisance because they make their homes among the plants. The collector should be on guard against the former, and is encouraged to adopt preventative measures as part of a regular gardening routine.

Before discussing the most frequently encountered pests and the measures to be taken to combat them, it must be pointed out that many pests exposed to chemical treatment develop, over several generations, resistance to a particular pesticide which enables them to shrug off further treatment. The solution then is not to increase the frequency or strength of the dosage, but to switch to a different pesticide. Where a number of remedies are available, it is advisable to alternate them to prevent the pests from building up immunity.

All chemicals are potentially hazardous if used negligently, and pesticides and fungicides should be handled with care. Always read the supplier's instructions carefully and follow them precisely. Use only the recommended dosage rates. Increasing the concentration is wasteful since it is unlikely to prove more effective against the pest than the correct strength. On the contrary, a more concentrated solution is quite likely to damage the plant and may also be dangerous for the user.

Mealy Bug

Mealy bugs are small creatures, up to about 0.2in (5mm) long, superficially similar in appearance to the familiar woodlouse. They are pink, but covered with a waxy secretion which makes them appear white to greyish. These pests are sap-suckers, attacking the softest tissue of the plant, particularly near the growing point. They reproduce from eggs laid in waxy cocoons having the appearance of small pieces of cotton-wool. These cocoons are often positioned at the junction between stem and branch or leaf, around the base of offsets, between the tubercles and ribs of cacti or between the leaves of rosette succulents. Frequent inspection is recommended, followed by prompt action if the pests are found, as they multiply very rapidly and a severe infestation can destroy the plant.

The bugs' waxy coating, being water-repellent, is the main protection against pesticide sprays. The coating is soluble in alcohol, so a convenient way of dealing with a small number of pests is to touch them with a soft paintbrush dipped in methylated or surgical spirits. Caution should be used when the plant has a waxy coating or a powdery bloom, as the spirits will dissolve these to leave unsightly marks.

A serious infestation may be tackled by spraying with a solution of contact pesticide, to which a small amount of detergent has been added as a wetting agent. Suitable pesticides are those containing permethrin, malathion or pyrethrum. This should be repeated two or three times at fortnightly intervals to kill survivors or any newly hatched pests.

As part of a programme of preventative measures, the whole collection could be watered two or three times a year with a systemic insecticide containing dimethoate. This is absorbed into the sap, making all parts of the plant poisonous to sap-sucking pests.

Root Mealy Bug

Despite the similarity of name, root mealy bugs are different creatures from those described above. They are smaller, about 0.1in (2mm) long, and live on the roots and underground parts of the plant. They too are coated with wax and appear white in colour.

Root mealy bug is a more serious pest than mealy bug since it multiplies insidiously out of sight underground. Often the first indications of its presence are powdery white traces in the compost when a plant is removed from its pot. The pest appears to thrive in dry composts, multiplying rapidly, and has a miraculous ability to spread from pot to pot until the whole collection is infested. Because the roots are attacked, a heavy infestation may cause a plant to stop growing and look sickly. If an infestation is suspected, the plant should be tipped out of its pot or the compost scratched away from the base of the stem to confirm the presence of the pest.

Affected plants should be repotted. The old compost should be removed from the roots, which are then soaked in a solution of contact insecticide. The incorporation into the fresh compost of a soil insecticide containing diazinon or bromophos will deal with any pests hatching later. Since root mealy bug is also a sap-sucking pest, occasional watering with a systemic insecticide is a useful preventive measure.

Scale Insect

This pest, apparently quite common many years ago, is rarely encountered nowadays. As it may reappear, particularly if large old plants from neglected collections are introduced, it is included here.

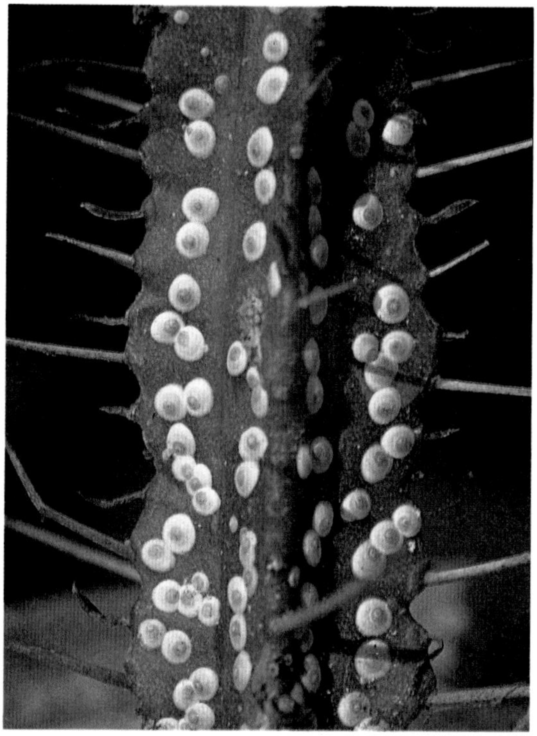

Fig 33 Scale insects can affect many types of plants, including succulents.

Scale insects are sap-sucking pests which are protected by a disc-shaped waxy scale. They attach themselves firmly to the surface of the plant, multiplying by producing eggs under the scale. This waxy scale makes the pests very resistant to contact pesticides, but they are susceptible to systemic insecticides.

Red Spider Mite

This is another insidious pest which can do a great deal of damage before it is detected. The name is misleading, as it is unrelated to the true spiders. It is reddish-brown in colour, extremely tiny and difficult to see with the naked eye.

Red spider mite thrives in warm, dry conditions, when it rapidly multiplies and spreads. It is particularly attracted to soft-bodied plants such as species of *Rebutia*, though it also appears to be selective. Often one plant will be heavily infested while another specimen of the same species growing alongside will be clear. The mite attacks the plant by piercing the skin and sucking the sap. Because of its small size and the number of creatures packed closely together, the result of a heavy infestation is a uniform browning of the epidermis. This is often the first indication of the presence of the mite. If, by the time the damage is noticed, the pests have moved on, it may be mistaken for scorch damage. A badly damaged plant is irretrievably ruined since the marking is permanent. If the growing point has been killed, it will be a long time before offsets have grown sufficiently to conceal the damage, though they may be removed and propagated to provide replacement plants. Even when the plant continues to grow, the dead tissue causes a constriction and the shape is distorted.

This is a pest that is best prevented from establishing itself, and a regime of watering with a systemic insecticide is advisable. Where the pest has established itself, a contact insecticide containing rotenone, malathion or pirimiphos-methyl is recommended. This pest is among the more difficult to eradicate, so several treatments may be necessary.

Sciarid Fly

The sciarid fly, also known as the mushroom fly, is a relative newcomer to the fauna of a succulent collection. Although an old enemy of the mushroom farmer, it appears to have spread to succulent plant collections with the introduction of peat-based composts. The adult form is a tiny black fly which tends to run about on the surface of the compost and, when it takes to the air, has a rather erratic flight. Its larvae, about ¼in (6mm) long, are white with black heads. They live in the compost where they feed on, among other material, plant roots. They also attack the tender tissue at the base of the stems of young seed lings.

The pests thrive in moist, warm conditions, which makes them particularly troublesome in seedtrays. Since they feed on organic material, a seed-raising compost containing only inorganic material will discourage them.

Should the pest be discovered among mature plants, a two-pronged attack is called for. The mature insects can be eliminated by a pyrethrum- or permethrin-based spray. The larvae are best tackled by soil pest insecticide containing diazinon or bromophos which can be stirred into the compost. Incorporating granules of these materials into the compost before sowing seed is an effective preventative measure.

Nematodes

These pests are also known as eelworms. Although not common pests in cultivation, when they do appear they can be difficult to eradicate. They occur in the soil and attack the roots of the plant. Once sufficient damage has been done to the roots, the plant ceases growth, and this is usually the first indication that anything is amiss.

Control is difficult, the usual approach being to add a soil insecticide such as diazinon, bromophos or gamma-HCH to the potting compost. The pest is sensitive to heat, and in the case of a particularly valuable plant, immersion of the roots in hot water (113 °F, 45 °C) for half an hour is recommended. Nematodes are easily spread from infected to fresh compost and breed rapidly, so urgent attention should be directed to dealing with a suspected infestation.

Aphids

Aphids of various kinds, greenfly, blackfly and whitefly, occasionally invade a greenhouse. In the protected environment, away from natural predators, they can multiply alarmingly. Usually they congregate on flower stems, where they are easily detected. As sap-sucking insects they succumb to systemic insecticides, but in general they are easily dealt with using any of the contact types.

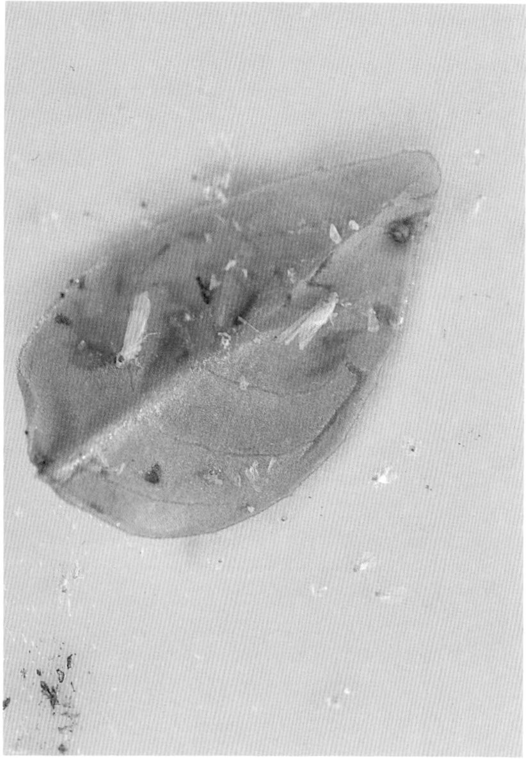

Fig 34 Whitefly are one of the commonest pests and can infest succulents.

Fig 35 Cactus with extensive scorch damage. This type of damage may be confused with that caused by red spider mite.

Other Pests

There are a number of other creatures not normally included in a list of pests of succulents, which turn up occasionally to cause extensive damage.

Slugs and snails prefer cool, damp places, but they are prepared to brave the arid conditions of a succulent house to enjoy a change of diet. They sometimes appear to have a built-in navigation system which guides them up the side of a greenhouse, through a ventilator and straight to the choicest plant inside. Even the soft-bodied slugs are able to avoid the fiercest spines to gouge out part of the body of a cactus, while tender succulent leaves are taken without inconvenience. A proprietary slug killer will solve this problem.

Caterpillars of a variety of butterflies and moths will sometimes enter a greenhouse to browse on succulent plant foliage. In southerly parts of Britain, one type of caterpillar has developed a liking for Echeverias. They enter the stem at ground level and munch their way upwards, giving no indication of their presence until leaves fall off the plant. Cutting through the stem reveals the hollow centre with the culprit curled up near the growing point.

Vine weevils can also be a problem. Their larvae enter the plant body at ground level and eat the flesh to leave no more than a hollow shell. The recommended treatment for both caterpillars and vine weevils is the application of a dust containing rotenone or a liquid containing permethrin.

Nuisances

In addition to the pests which attack succulent plants, there are several creatures which can cause a nuisance by invading a greenhouse, though they are less likely to be found among a living-room collection.

Ants enjoy warm conditions and sometimes try to establish a colony in a propagator or a large pot. Their nuisance value is in disturbing the roots and so checking the growth of the plants. As the nest is excavated the surplus soil is built up into a mound which may bury and smother small plants. Proprietary products which will eliminate them are readily available.

Spiders do a great deal of good by catching insect pests, but with the onset of winter they often make their way into the shelter of a greenhouse. Some of the larger kinds take up residence among the pots and drape the neighbouring plants with dense, sticky webs that are difficult to remove. Recognising their beneficial services, it is kindest to catch them by hand and release them at a distance from the greenhouse.

Leaf-cutter bees are fascinating creatures which live solitary lives. To reproduce they manufacture a nest from rolled-up fragments of leaf or flower petals tucked into a suitable crevice. This may be a small hole in the compost at the base of a plant, in which case the subsequent root disturbance may cause a check in the growth. Fortunately they are rare visitors to our greenhouses, so can usually be tolerated for their entertainment value.

Field mice occasionally make a home among a collection of succulents and can be something of a nuisance. They are omnivorous and are not to know that the juicy cactus fruit on which they breakfasted was something special and that the owner had been waiting for it to ripen before gathering the seeds. Mice are attractive little creatures that can be captured in humane traps and released into the wild, well away from the garden.

Unless ventilator and door openings are screened, birds may find their way into a greenhouse. They normally pose no threat to mature plants if left to their own devices, but they may become entangled with hook-spined cacti if attempts are made to chase them out. They can, however, cause havoc by searching for insects and grubs among trays of seedlings, which they will uproot and scatter to all corners of the greenhouse. Excluding them is a simpler approach than clearing up after a visit.

FUNGAL DISEASES

Among the problems facing the collector, fungal disease is possibly the most disheartening. Whether it is damping-off disease among a batch of seedlings or one of the other diseases attacking a mature plant, it proceeds remorselessly to its conclusion within a short period of time. In many cases, by the time it is recognised it is beyond cure. Prophylactic measures are more rewarding than desperate attempts to check the spread of an established outbreak.

Damping-Off Disease

This is a fungus which attacks young seedlings. It thrives in the warm, moist conditions required for seed germination, and spreads rapidly. When attacked, the seedlings lose their rigidity, becoming soft and watery, and quickly collapse. Within a day or two the whole crop may be lost.

The use of a sterilised mineral-based seed compost, which has been treated before seeds are sown with a fungicide containing copper sulphate, chinosol or benomyl, will discourage the onset of the disease. It may appear after the seeds have germinated, from fungus spores in the atmosphere. Spraying with a fungicide may check the spread of the disease to healthy seedlings, which are then best transplanted into fresh sterilised compost. It will not save those seedlings already infected.

Basal Rots

These diseases can occur in mature plants if the compost is insufficiently drained or the plant is given too much water during the part of the year when it should be resting. The fungus enters the

Fig 36 Mildew can be effectively dealt with by the use of liquids, powders or smoke cones.

roots and proceeds upwards through the vascular tissue to the growing point. Often the plant will appear healthy, apart from a tendency to wobble at the base when handled. Eventually the diseased tissue extends to the skin and appears as black or brown patches at the base of the stem.

Halting the disease calls for drastic treatment. The plant stem should be cut through above the affected region and the vascular tissue carefully inspected. If orange or brown spots are present, further cuts should be made until the tissue appears clean and healthy. The cut surface should then be dusted with a fungicide powder and dried for a few days, after which the stem can be treated as a cutting.

Black Spot

Some succulents, in particular Stapeliads, develop irregular black marks on the stems. Cutting through the stem usually reveals that the disease has propagated through the vascular tissue, which appears black in colour. There is little prospect of saving a plant in which the disease has become established, unless healthy stems can be found to treat as cuttings.

It is considered that this disease enters the plant body through damaged roots, perhaps following attack by soil-based pests such as root mealy bug. A regime of watering at intervals of a few weeks with a systemic fungicide containing benomyl will help the plant to resist infection.

Mildew

In the autumn, as the weather turns colder and damper, mildews may appear on flower stems and tender young growth. These are not only unsightly but potentially dangerous as they may spread. In those conditions there is some reluctance to spray the plants with liquids, and dusting with a fungicide powder or with green sulphur may be more appropriate. Alternatively, it is possible to obtain smoke cones containing tecnazene: when burnt the fumes are dissipated to all parts of the greenhouse.

CULTURAL ERRORS

There are other reasons for plants failing to thrive, and some of these have been discussed in Chapter 2 with regard to cultivation. They are frequently linked with the problems described above. Often errors in cultivation weaken the plants and make them more susceptible to attack by pests and diseases. Treating the apparent problem without considering the possibility that cultivation errors may have initiated it is likely to lead to the problem recurring.

Cold damage may occur in extreme weather. Even though the average temperature is satisfac-

Fig 37 Plants displayed in a healthy greenhouse environment.

tory, there may be cold spots close to the glass, at low level or where draughts occur. Damage caused by cold often manifests itself as a lightening in the colour of stems or the appearance of orange spots on the bodies of cacti. In extreme circumstances where temperatures have fallen to a level allowing the tender growing points to be frozen, this may become apparent many weeks later as browning of the stem tip.

Early in the year, when overnight frosts may be followed by clear, sunny days, the greenhouse temperature may rise to unacceptable levels if the ventilation is insufficient. Tender young growth may be scorched. There is also the risk that moving plants to a different position, perhaps after repotting, and turning them round relative to the incident sunlight, may encourage scorching. Scorching is indicated by a browning of the epidermis, but this can be confused with red spider mite damage. Close inspection with a powerful lens (×10) is advisable before jumping to conclusions.

CHAPTER 4

Propagation

For most growers, only a short time elapses between purchase of the first plant and realisation that there are other ways of adding to a collection. The most obvious, and most satisfying, is by raising plants from seed. There are others though. Cactophiles are generous folk, and when the novice makes contact with fellow enthusiasts, he or she will almost certainly be given cuttings and offsets and will be faced with the need to persuade them to form roots. There will perhaps be occasions when, as the consequence of attack by disease or pests, a favourite plant is reduced to a handful of unrooted fragments. The grower will then hope to root the fragments or to graft them successfully to save the plant. There is also a facet of the hobby that appeals to some growers: the creation of new forms by hybridisation. These aspects will now be discussed.

SEED RAISING

Raising plants from seed is probably the most rewarding part of the hobby. It has the attraction

Fig 38 Lobivia pentlandii v. larae.

that it is an inexpensive way of increasing one's collection since a packet of seed costing much less than a plant may, with moderate skill, produce many plants. By raising them from seed, the grower has total control at all times and his or her skill can result in perfect plants, free of blemishes. The greatest attraction, however, must be following the plant through all stages from seed to seedling to mature plant producing flowers and eventually seed: the complete cycle of growth.

The first necessity for success is attention to hygiene. Young seedlings are vulnerable to attack by pests and fungal diseases and, since they are initially very small, such attacks may destroy them before being recognised. A regime of preventative measures is desirable.

It is essential that the seeds should be viable, and here there is a problem. Seed offered commercially will have been imported, either collected in the habitat or produced artificially from plants cultivated for the purpose, and may be more than a year old before it is sown. This is of little consequence in the case of most succulent seeds, but there are some which have a short period of viability. If it is possible to obtain freshly harvested seed, success is more easily achieved.

The fruits of many succulent plants dry out and release the seeds by splitting. In some, the seeds are retained in a pulp which adheres to the seeds, only being removed by passage through the gut of an animal or bird. It is likely that the seeds to be sown are contaminated by fragments of pulp, skin and other material. There may also be crushed seeds or some that are empty husks. Not only is it pointless to sow this material, but it is a potential source of infection.

If the seeds are spread out on a sheet of white paper and examined through a lens, it will be possible to pick out the larger fragments of extraneous material. Since most seeds are approximately spherical in shape, by keeping the paper almost horizontal and gently tapping it, the seeds can be encouraged to roll off, leaving the dust and small fragments behind. The clean seeds can then be mixed with a little seed-dressing powder containing captan as a prophylactic against fungal diseases.

The compost used should be permeable, low in nutrients and sterile. Commercial composts are usually advertised as being sterile, but with the small amounts required for seedraising it is worth the extra effort to ensure this. Put an open biscuit-tin of compost in the oven, where it can be heated to about 212 °F (100 °C) for fifteen minutes. To improve the permeability of the compost, perlite or crushed grit may be added. After mixing, the compost should be neutral to slightly acid. To combat sciarid fly, which may be attracted to the seed container at a later date, a granular soil insecticide containing diazinon or bromophos may be incorporated into the compost after sterilisation.

Depending on the quantities of each kind of seed to be sown, containers may be selected. Be optimistic: assume that all the seeds will germinate and that they will remain in the pots until large enough to be handled comfortably. Allow space for their development, and do not sow into pots that are too small. It is easier to control conditions in larger pots, and overcrowding of the young seedlings may lead to distortion of their bodies. The containers should be sterile. If possible use new pots, but otherwise ensure that they are thoroughly cleaned and disinfected.

The pots are filled to the top, then tapped on a rigid surface to settle the compost, leaving the surface level and a few millimetres below the rim. The compost should not be compacted. The filled pots are then watered by standing them in a shallow container of sterile water, preferably rainwater that has been boiled and allowed to cool. When the top surface is moist, the pots are removed from the container and allowed to drain for a few minutes. They are then ready to receive the seeds.

The seeds should be sprinkled on to the surface, making every effort to distribute them uniformly. Holding the open packet close to the pot and gently tapping it encourages the seeds to trickle out in a steady stream. If some seeds congregate in clumps, they may be separated using

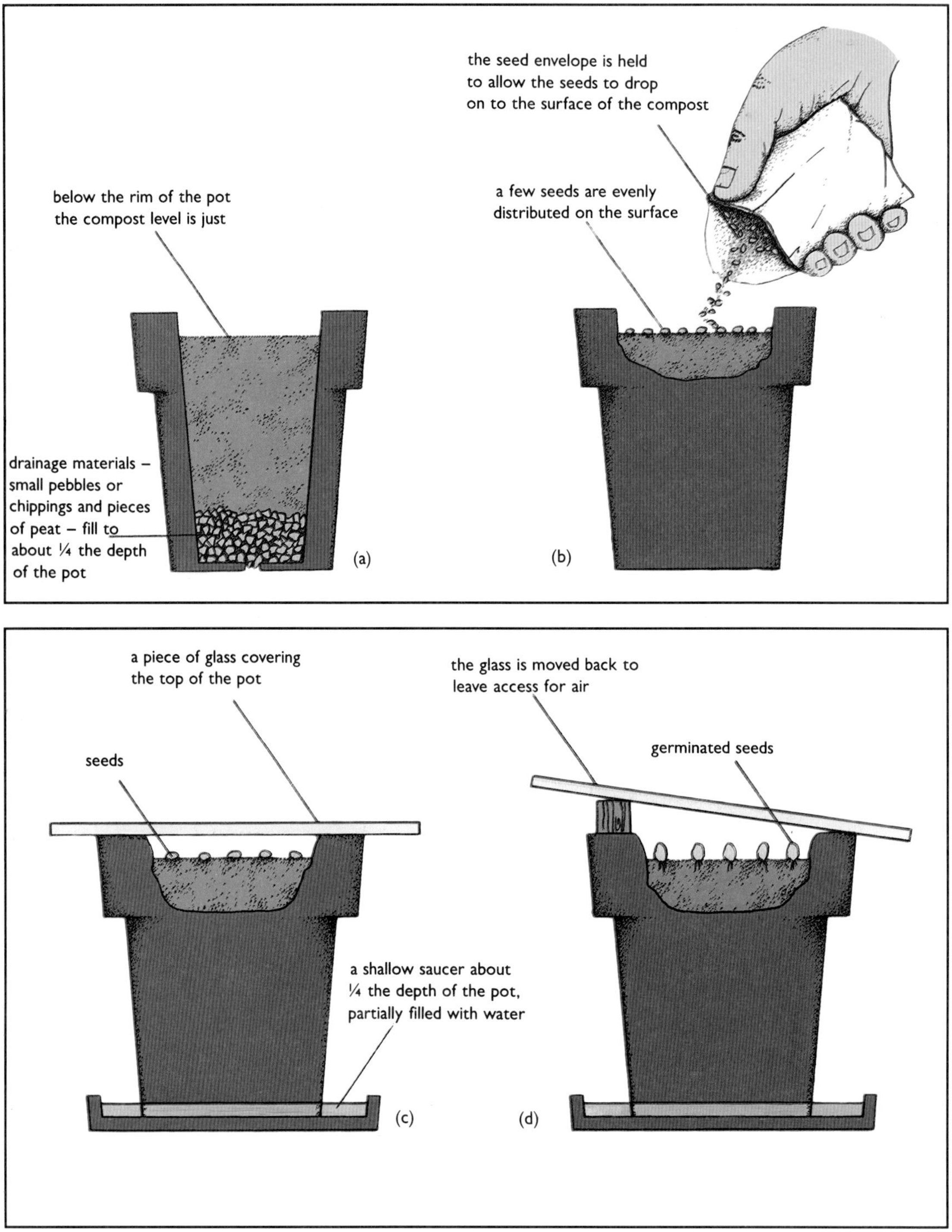

Fig 39 Seed raising; (a) prepare a pot using compost and drainage material (b) distribute the seeds evenly over the surface (c) cover the top of the pot with a piece of glass to aid humidity and warmth (d) once the seeds have germinated move the glass back to allow access for air.

the point of a penknife or similar implement. The object is to give each seedling space to develop without interference from its neighbours.

The smaller seeds should not be buried since light aids germination. The larger seeds may be gently pressed into the surface or just covered with a thin layer of crushed grit or similar material. In the case of large, flat seeds that are relatively fragile (such as those of Aloes or Stapeliads), it may be better to use the point of a knife to make recesses in the compost, in which the seeds may be placed edgewise using tweezers.

To obtain good germination it is necessary to provide warmth and humidity. The ideal temperature for most succulents is about 75–85 °F (25–30 °C) during the day, falling slightly lower at night. To achieve this temperature very early in the year – some growers like to sow seeds as early as January – supplementary heating is required. Commercial propagators with thermostatic control are available, at a price. Simple ones, large enough to accommodate a dozen or so 3in (75mm) pots, cost a few pounds. The competent handyman may be able to construct a simple propagator, incorporating a thermostatically controlled soil-heating cable, but particular attention must be paid to safety aspects. Those unable to provide such conditions are advised to delay sowing until March or April, when solar heating should be adequate.

The other requirement for good germination is to maintain the compost uniformly moist at all times. If it is allowed to dry out while the seeds are germinating, they will perish. To keep the compost moist, the pot may be stood in a shallow container in a few millimetres of water, which is topped up when necessary. The use of a piece of capillary matting which is always kept wet is another way of solving the problem of keeping the compost moist but not waterlogged. It is advisable not to water seedtrays by means of a watering-can, though an occasional mist spraying is beneficial. Needless to say, the water used should be sterile.

A technique that has been used successfully by a number of growers is to enclose the seed pot in a sealed polythene bag. By this means the water evaporating from the compost condenses on the bag and is returned to moisten the compost again. A uniform humidity is maintained, and the seedlings are allowed to remain in this sterile microclimate until large enough for pricking out.

Initially, light shading should be provided. Usually a single sheet of tissue paper is sufficient. This is draped over the pots in such a way that it does not touch the compost and does not have lowspots from which condensed water will drip on to the surface of the compost.

Given the conditions described above, success should follow. Some kinds of seed may germinate within two or three days, while some will take longer. Once germinated, there is a danger that seedlings will become elongated if they remain shaded, so daily examination is essential. The newly germinated seedlings should not be moved immediately into full light, but the shading should be reduced over a period of several days by gradually moving the covering further away. After about a week the seedlings should be in good light but not directly exposed to full sunlight. Only after development of recognisable though miniature forms of the adult plants should they be exposed to the sun.

After germination of the seedlings and their exposure to the normal greenhouse environment, it is essential to be on guard against attack by pests and diseases. The most likely enemies are damping-off disease, which may be combated by a suitable fungicide, and sciarid fly, the larvae of which can destroy a crop of seedlings within a few days (*see* Chapter 2).

Depending on their rate of growth, the seedlings will eventually need to be pricked out. This may be necessary within a few months in the case of some of the faster-growing kinds, while others may remain in the seed pots for a full season. When the time comes, it is advisable to have the compost in the seed pot just moist. It may then be carefully emptied out of the pot and gently crumbled to disentangle the seedlings with

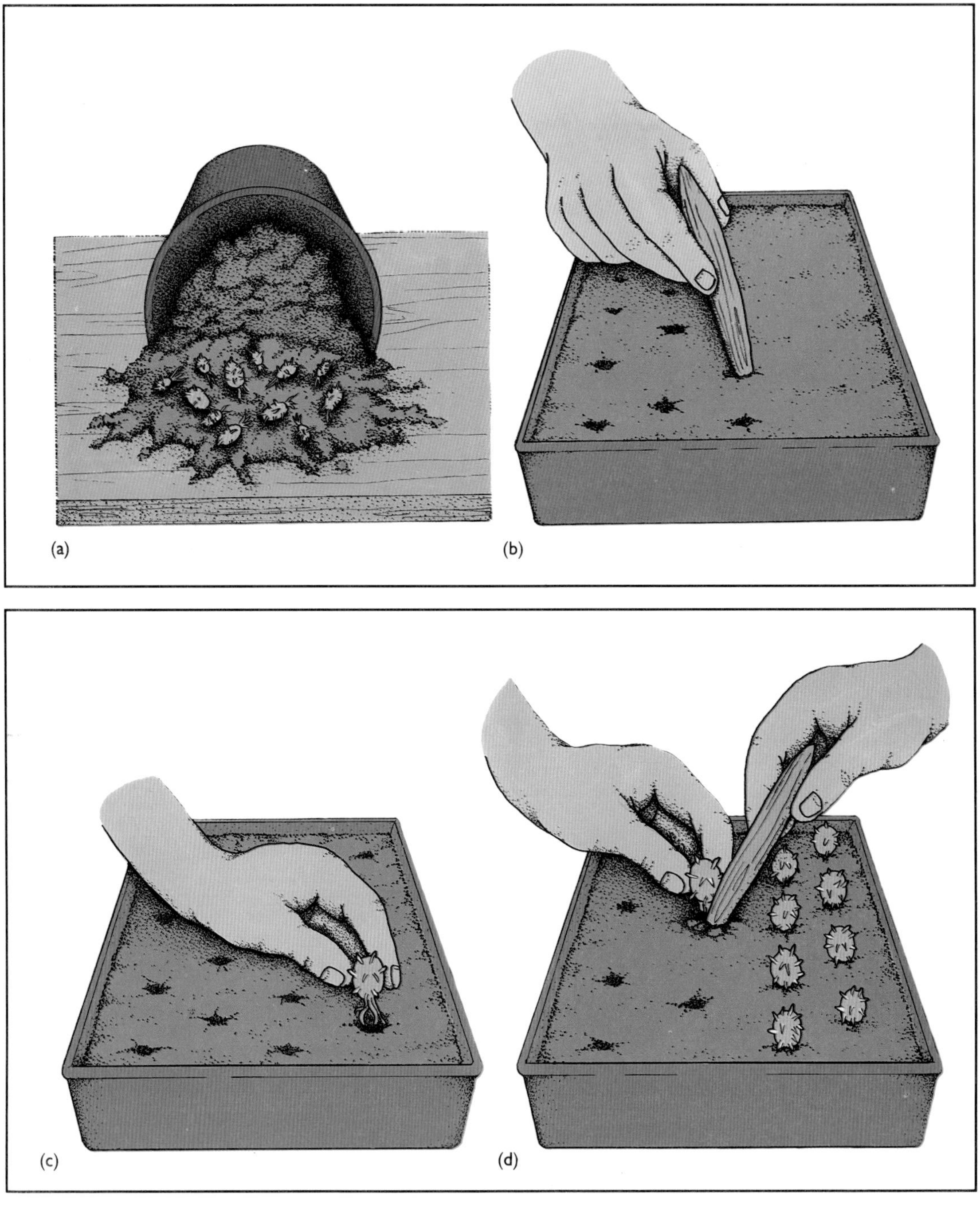

Fig 40 Pricking out seedlings; (a) gently tip the pot on to its side on a work-bench to enable the seeds to be removed easily (b) use a dibber to make holes in the compost in seed tray, to accommodate the seedlings (c) insert the roots of the seedlings into the holes (d) once the seedlings are in place, with their bodies resting on the surface of the compost, gently firm the soil with a dibber.

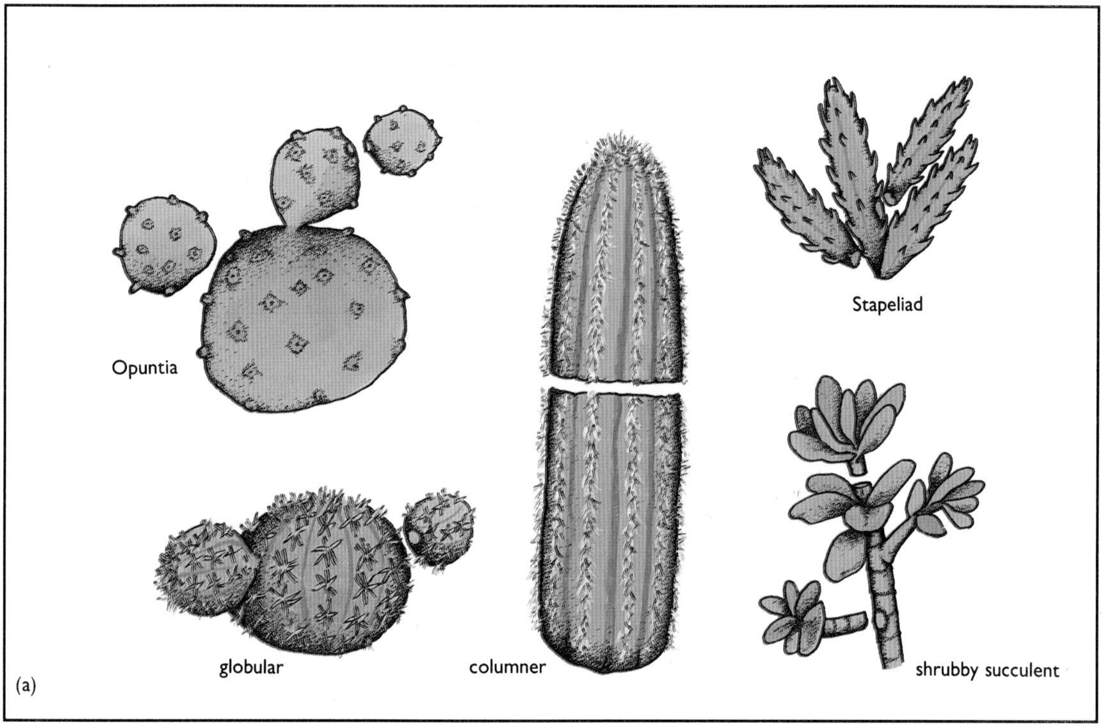

Fig 41 These illustrations show (a) where to take cuttings from a plant, and (b) how they will look once they have been taken.

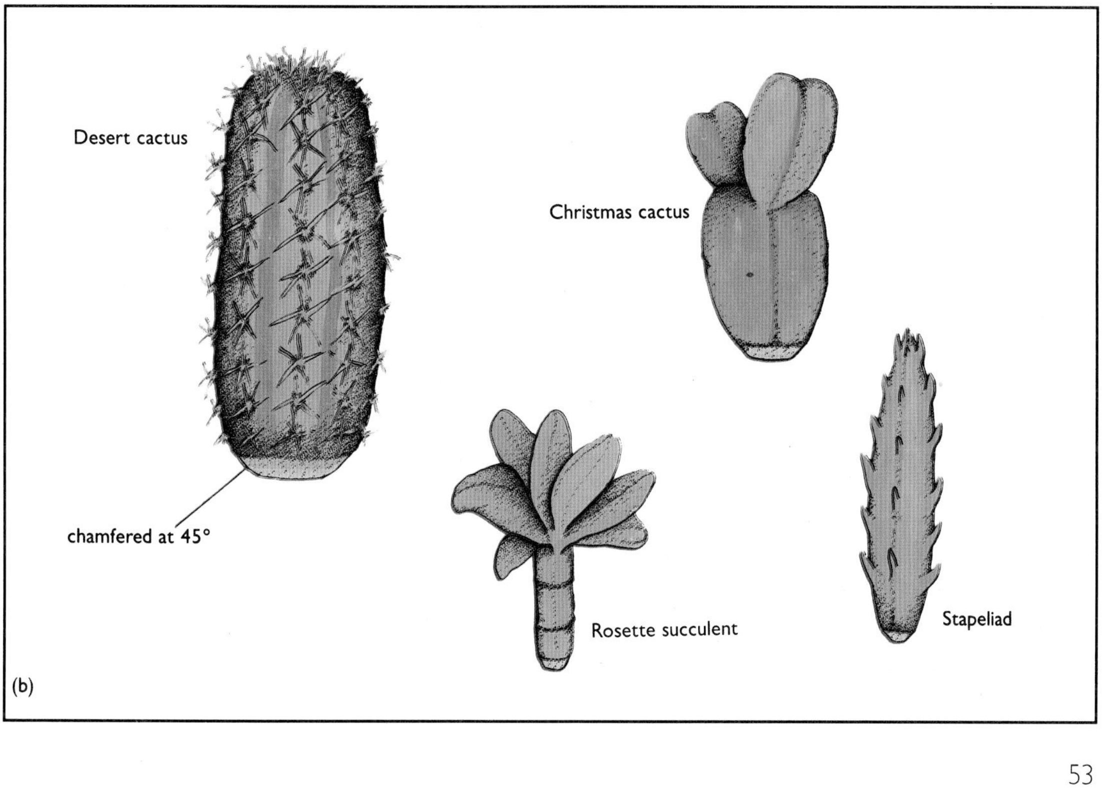

minimal damage to their roots. This is usually preferable to digging the individual seedlings from the seed pot. Leave as much compost as possible adhering to the roots when transferring the seedlings to fresh compost. For some reason, young seedlings seem to grow better in company, so planting a number together in a seedtray or pot is preferable to potting them singly in small pots. After pricking out, it is advisable to be cautious with watering for a week or two, to enable damaged roots to heal and the seedlings to establish themselves.

CUTTINGS

Offsets and stem cuttings taken from branching plants provide a convenient way of sharing a favourite plant with other enthusiasts, and if they are removed with care the damage to the mother plant is minimal. The process also provides a means of producing a healthy replacement from a diseased or damaged specimen. In many cases, plants that have grown too tall for their allotted space can be beheaded. The top can be rooted while the decapitated stump often produces offsets which in turn can be removed and rooted.

Whenever possible, a complete branch should be taken as the cutting. If part of the stem is taken, the cut surface is much greater in area and more susceptible to fungal attack. Ideally the cut should be made at the 'neck' where the branch joins the main stem. A clean and very sharp blade should be used – a razor blade is ideal – to limit the amount of damage to both cutting and mother plant. Where it is only possible to cut across the stem, the cut should be chamfered to reduce shrinkage of the cut surface.

Although not essential, it is a wise precaution to dust the cut surface with a fungicide to combat fungal spores that may be present in the atmosphere. The cutting should then be placed in an airy situation, but not in full sun, until the cut surface has formed a callus. If the cut surface is small, this may take only a few hours (say overnight) but if it has been necessary to cut across a stem of large diameter, callus formation may take several days.

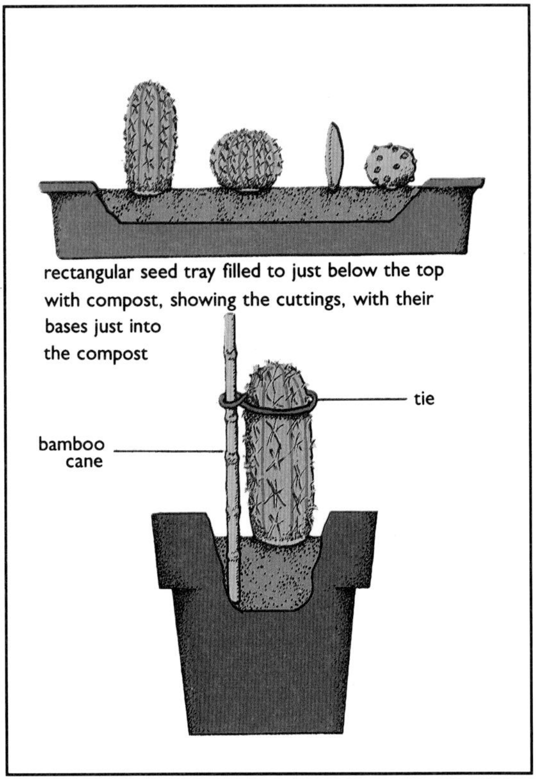

Fig 42 Cuttings in the process of rooting. Larger cuttings can be steadied by a cane.

The compost used for rooting cuttings should be sterile and should contain little nutrient. A 'poor' compost encourages the plant to develop a sturdy root system. It should be just moist and should be kept in that condition until the cutting has an adequate system of roots. The cutting is planted with its cut surface about ⅛in (3mm) below the compost surface. Globular cactus offsets and succulent rosettes are no problem, but taller cuttings may be top-heavy and tend to fall over. They can be stabilised by tying them to short supports inserted more deeply into the compost. The use of a rooting hormone is usually unnecessary, but will do no harm as it contains a fungicide.

While rooting, the cuttings should be kept in slight shade to prevent dehydration. If warmth can be provided, particularly in the form of bot-

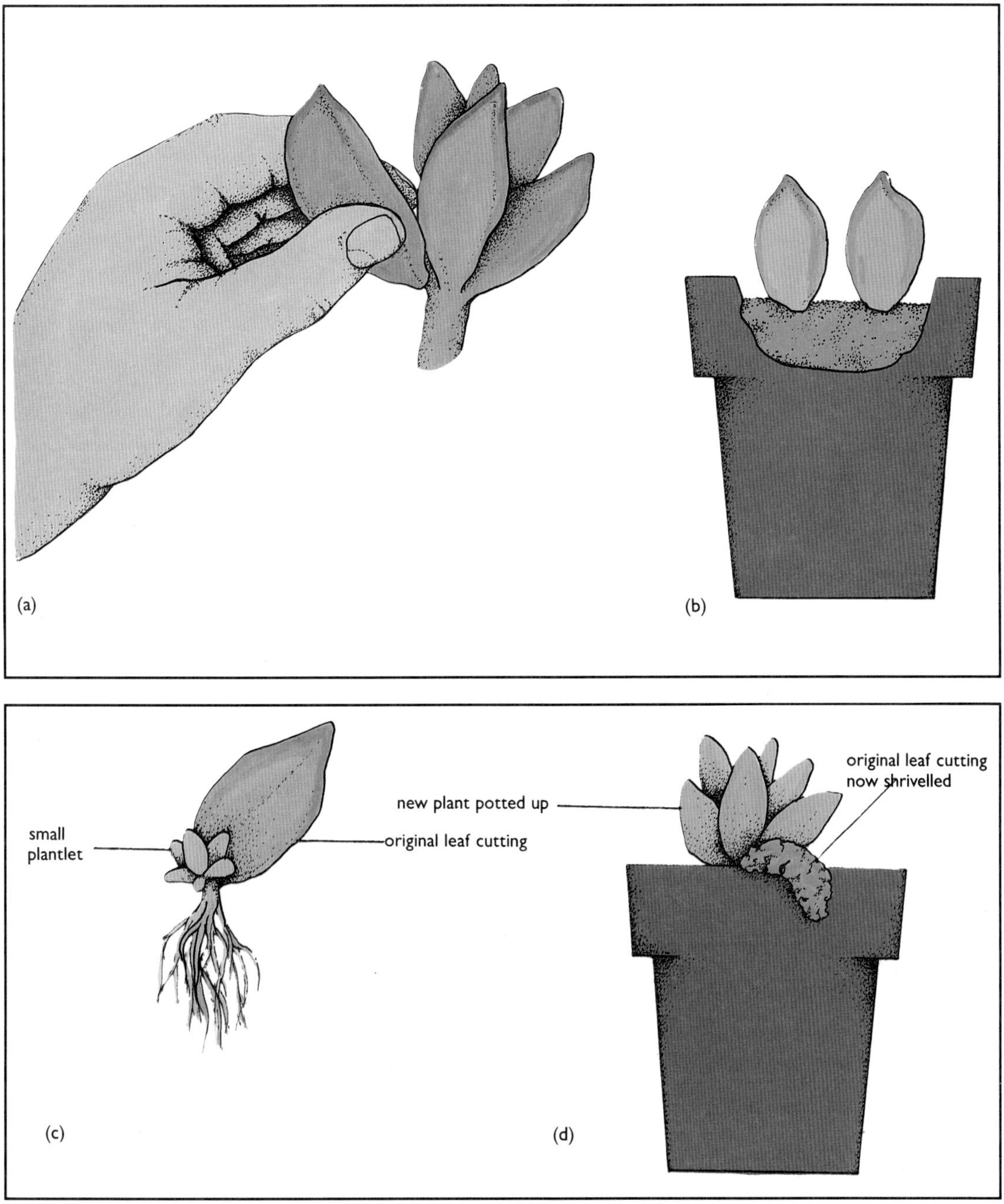

Fig 43 Leaf cuttings; (a) detach a side leaf from the plant (b) position each leaf with its base just into the compost (c) the small plantlet will start to root and grow (d) finally the new plant will establish itself.

tom heat from a soil-heating cable, the process of rooting is accelerated. To prevent excessive shrivelling, a mist spray may be used. Rooting may occur within a few days, or may take many months: cuttings taken during the period of growth are usually more successful than those taken at other times. Once roots have formed, the plant is potted in the usual compost and treated as any other repotted plant.

Many of the leaf succulents can be propagated from single leaves. Usually it is necessary to take the complete leaf, but there are some that will produce a cluster of plantlets from a fragment of leaf. The leaves to be used as cuttings should be selected carefully whenever possible. They should be plump, healthy and not beginning to die. Usually the outermost leaves of a rosette are not suitable, and leaves should be taken from nearer to the centre. The small leaves produced on the flower stems of some succulents (for example, *Echeveria*) provide a fruitful source of new plants. This method of propagation is most suitable for many members of the Crassulaceae (*Adromischus*, *Crassula*, *Echeveria*, *Pachyphytum*, etc.), the Liliaceae (*Gasteria*, *Haworthia*) and some others, but it is always worth experimenting.

It is usually unnecessary to wait for the leaves to develop a callus. They may be dipped into a rooting hormone and laid on the surface of the compost or inserted just below it. Sometimes the leaves will rot, sometimes they will shrivel, but often they will produce plantlets at their bases which can be removed when sufficiently large.

GRAFTING

Grafted cacti are more popular on the Continent than they are in Britain, where they tend to be regarded as evidence of lack of skill in cultivation. It is true that it is often easier to grow a 'touchy' plant when grafted on to a vigorous root stock, but this is only part of the story. In order to propagate rare plants more rapidly, nurseries sometimes resort to grafting offsets or seedlings on to more vigorous kinds. This increases the rate of growth, so that novelties reach the market-place more rapidly than if grown naturally. These composite plants, comprising a tall stem topped by a globular body, have received the derogatory appellation 'lollipop' and many purchasers immediately set about decapitating them and rooting the tops.

Apart from commercial considerations, there are good reasons for grafting. Some species that are particularly difficult on their own roots can be grown successfully when grafted. Slow-growing plants that would normally take many years to reach maturity can be grafted as minute seedlings and persuaded to flower within a few months. The freak forms containing little or no chlorophyll, which would not survive on their own roots, can be grown as grafts. Most importantly perhaps, the possession of skill in grafting may enable the grower to save a valued plant that would otherwise be lost. The technique of grafting is most commonly used for cacti, less frequently for some of the other stem succulents (*Euphorbia*, Stapeliads), and is not suitable for rosette plants.

The technique replaces the stem tip of a vigorously growing plant (the stock) with part of another plant (the scion) such that the two unite and continue to grow as an entity. The scion may be an offset, the upper part of a seedling or the tip of a stem. It is possible to graft other fragments, for example a single tubercle, but such applications are unusual and will not be described here. Successful grafting requires some knowledge of the internal structure of the stem, so this will be described first.

If a transverse cut is made through the stem of a cactus, inspection of the cut surface will reveal a 'core' in the form of an annulus of fibrous tissue. This is the vascular tissue, the artery carrying nutrients through the stem. The diameter of this ring of vascular tissue varies with the diameter of the stem and also with the type of cactus. In some species the ring is only about ⅛in (3mm) in diameter, in others the diameter is considerably

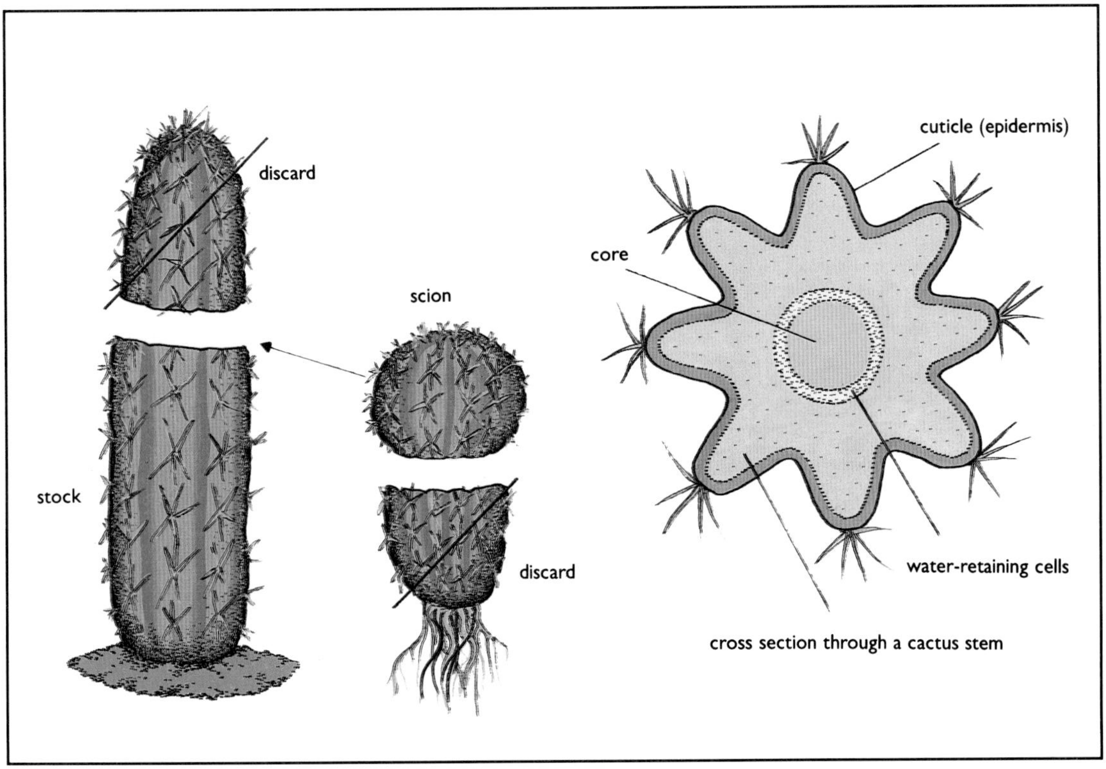

Fig 44 General terms that are applied to grafting.

greater, though the width of the ring may still be only about 1/8in.

In principle, grafting requires that the vascular tissue of the stock and scion should be held in contact until union has taken place. In practice, there is a little more to it than that. It is desirable that both stock and scion should be growing vigorously. The optimum time for grafting is the early part of the growing season, between April and June for most cacti, but it may be necessary to try grafting to save a plant fragment in mid-winter. Ideally, the diameters of the two rings of vascular tissue should be the same, so that union can take place over the whole area. If this is not the case, it will be necessary to offset the scion on the stock so that as much as possible of the vascular tissue is aligned, when union will take place only over that limited area.

There are several types of graft, of which the most commonly employed is the flat graft. In this type the two components are cut through to produce mating surfaces perpendicular to the longitudinal axes of the stems. A very sharp implement, such as a scalpel or razor blade, should be used, and this should be dipped into surgical spirit to sterilise it before making each cut. The cut surfaces should be flat and without any torn areas that might interfere with the union. To counteract the natural tendency of the cut tissue to shrink, which would separate the surfaces, the edges should be trimmed to produce a small chamfer. The cut surfaces are then brought into contact, ensuring that the vascular tissue is aligned correctly.

For union to take place it is essential that the surfaces are held firmly together for several days. This is most easily done by supporting a small piece of glass in such a way that it rests on top of the scion. Small pebbles placed on the glass provide sufficient pressure to maintain contact between the scion and the stock. The grafted plant is kept in the shade for a few days until union has taken place. The glass is then removed and the plant kept moist to encourage uptake of water.

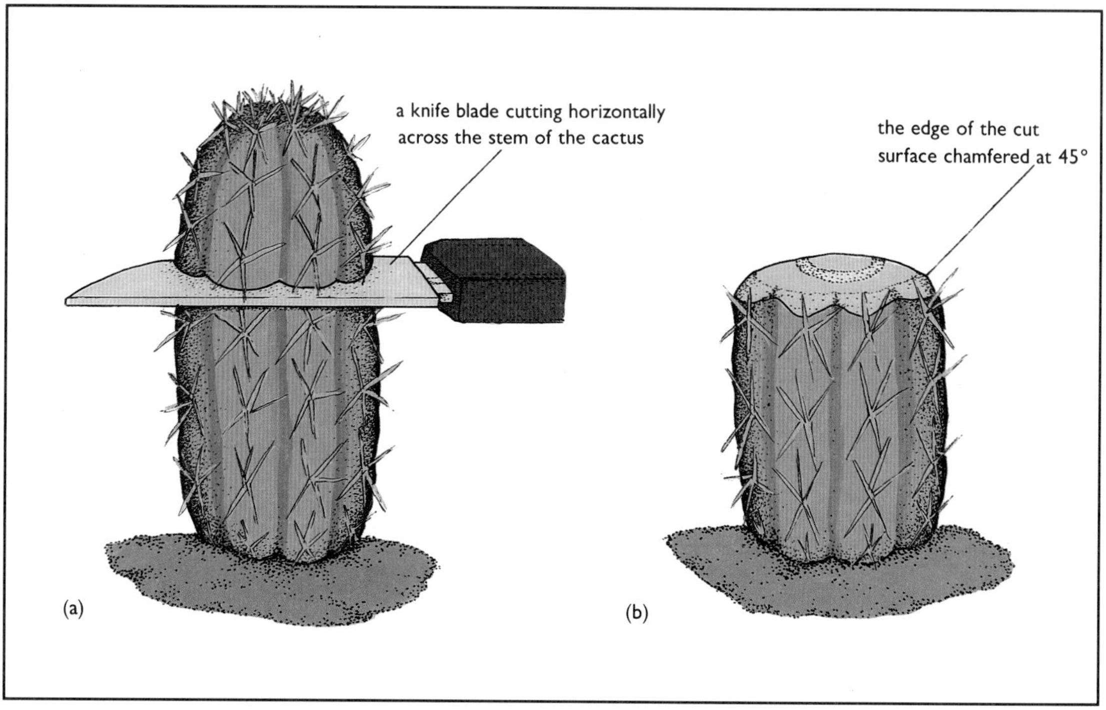

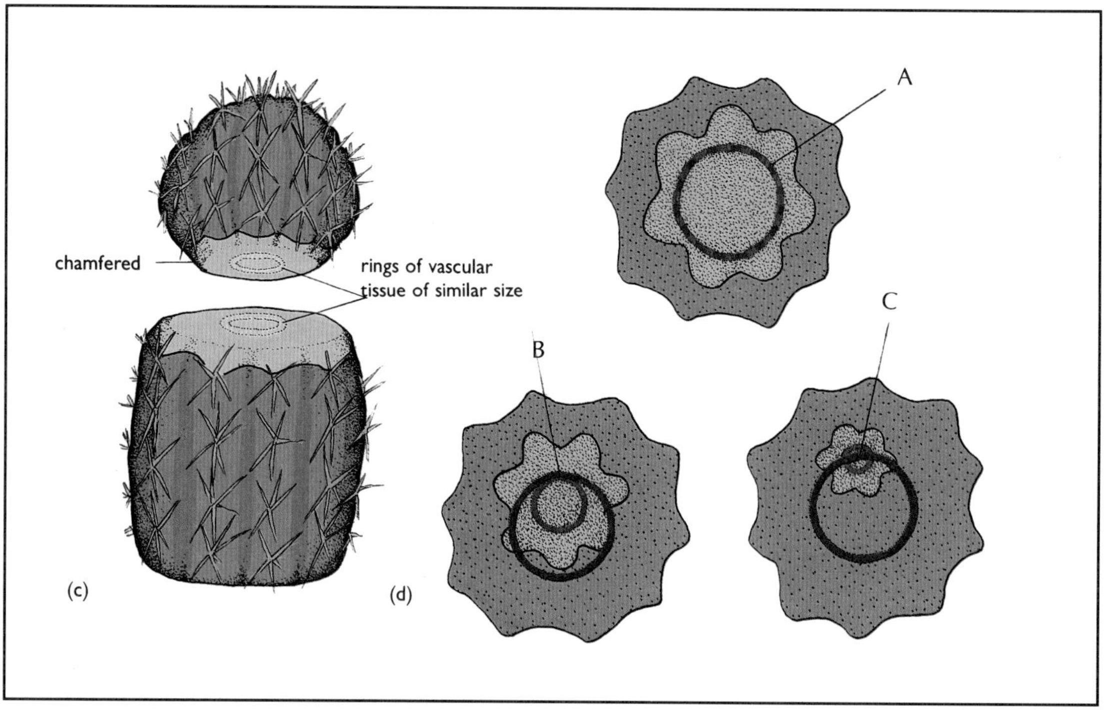

Fig 45 The flat graft; (a) cutting the plant (b) chamfering the edge of the cut surface (c) grafting the two parts together (d) cross-sections of the stock (blue) and scion (red), to show the matching of vascular tissue; top shows the perfect match, bottom left shows a smaller scion and bottom right shows a very small scion positioned at a point on the vascular tissue.

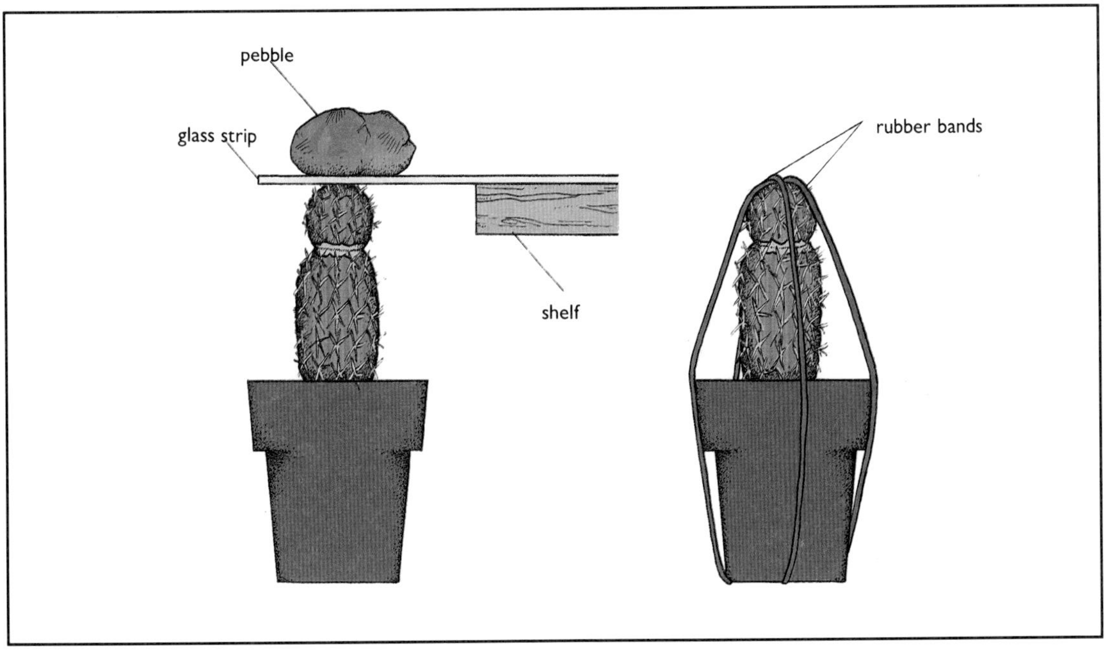

Fig 46 Two methods of holding the graft together in order to unite the stock and scion.

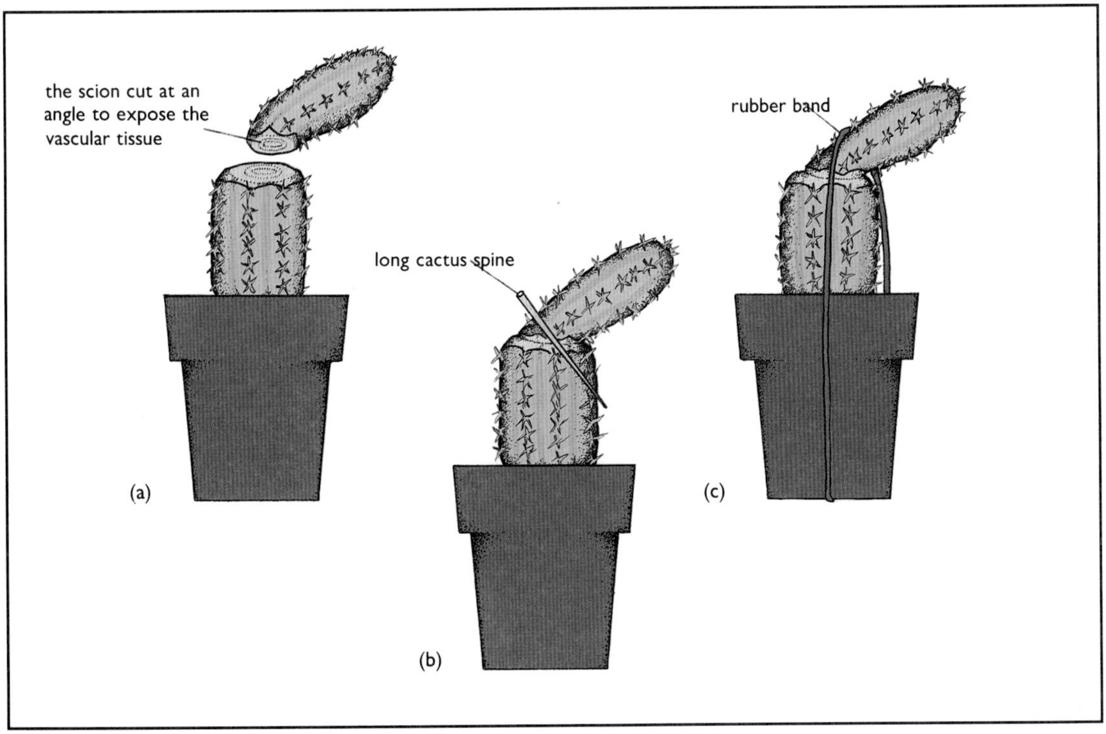

Fig 47 The side graft; (a) the positioning of the graft (b) the use of a sterilised spine to hold the graft (c) or alternatively the use of a rubber band to maintain the join.

When watering it is important to keep water away from the cut surfaces until they have formed a callus, otherwise infection may destroy the graft.

A variant of the flat graft, though not so frequently used, is the side graft. This is sometimes more convenient for cacti having a pendent habit. For side grafting, the cuts on both scion and stock are made at an angle rather than perpendicular to the axis. Maintaining pressure between the two components is more difficult, but binding them together with raffia or soft string is possible.

The most suitable stocks are the sturdier and more vigorous types such as *Echinopsis* and *Trichocereus*, though almost any cactus can be used. Avoid the tender types such as *Hylocereus* and *Myrtillocactus*, sometimes used by commercial growers. These often succumb to cold though the scion is perfectly hardy. When grafting other stem succulents, choose sturdy stocks of related species. It is no good trying to graft a Euphorbia on to a cactus, for example.

Sometimes short segments of such epiphytic cacti as the familiar 'Christmas Cactus' are grafted on to a tall stem (often of *Pereskia*), producing a standard plant which displays the blossoms to advantage. Because the stems of the epiphyte are broad and flat, a different type of graft is employed. This is the cleft graft. The base of the scion, usually a short length of two or three segments of stem, is trimmed to a wedge shape by removing a sliver of tissue from both faces, thus exposing the vascular tissue. The stock is prepared by first removing the tip by cutting the stem perpendicular to its axis, and then making a wedge-shaped incision to expose the vascular tissue. The scion is then inserted into the incision in such a way that the vascular tissue is in contact, and the joint is bound with soft string. Some growers employ a clothes-peg to hold the graft, but care must be taken not to damage the tender stems. If it is found that binding causes the scion to be forced out of the incision, it may be retained by pinning with a sterile cactus spine or splinter of wood. Do not use metal pins, which will corrode and cause infection of the union.

HYBRIDISATION

This is another topic attracting a reaction from many growers, who vehemently maintain that there is a sufficient diversity among the true species to render the creation of hybrids superfluous. This is, however, a somewhat blinkered view. No doubt most of those who oppose the creation of succulent plant hybrids grow hybrid roses, fuchsias and chrysanthemums. It is also likely that those who claim to grow only true species are unknowingly cultivating many hybrids!

Hybrids (crosses) are not only man-made. Some, though not a large number, occur in the wild. To produce a hybrid it is necessary to have two specimens of different but related species in flower at the same time. Pollen must be transferred from the male sex organ (anther) of one flower to the female sex organ (stigma) of the other. Pollination is usually performed by an animal agency which may be a bee, wasp, fly, butterfly, moth, bird or bat. One might assume that in the wild this process would occur frequently, but Nature adopts some cunning ways to prevent this happening. Closely related species do not usually occur in the same locality, but are geographically separated. Where related plants do grow in close proximity, their flowering periods tend not to coincide, or they employ different pollinators. By such means the purity of the species is maintained and miscegenation occurs only infrequently.

In cultivation, the situation is different. Plants that would grow many miles apart sit cheek by jowl on the staging. There is a great variety of insect visitors attracted to the flowers, which may include several capable of effecting pollen transfer, and in addition there may be the grower armed with a paintbrush as a substitute pollinator. Consequently, seed collected from cultivated plants often produces hybrid seedlings.

While chance hybrids are often almost in-

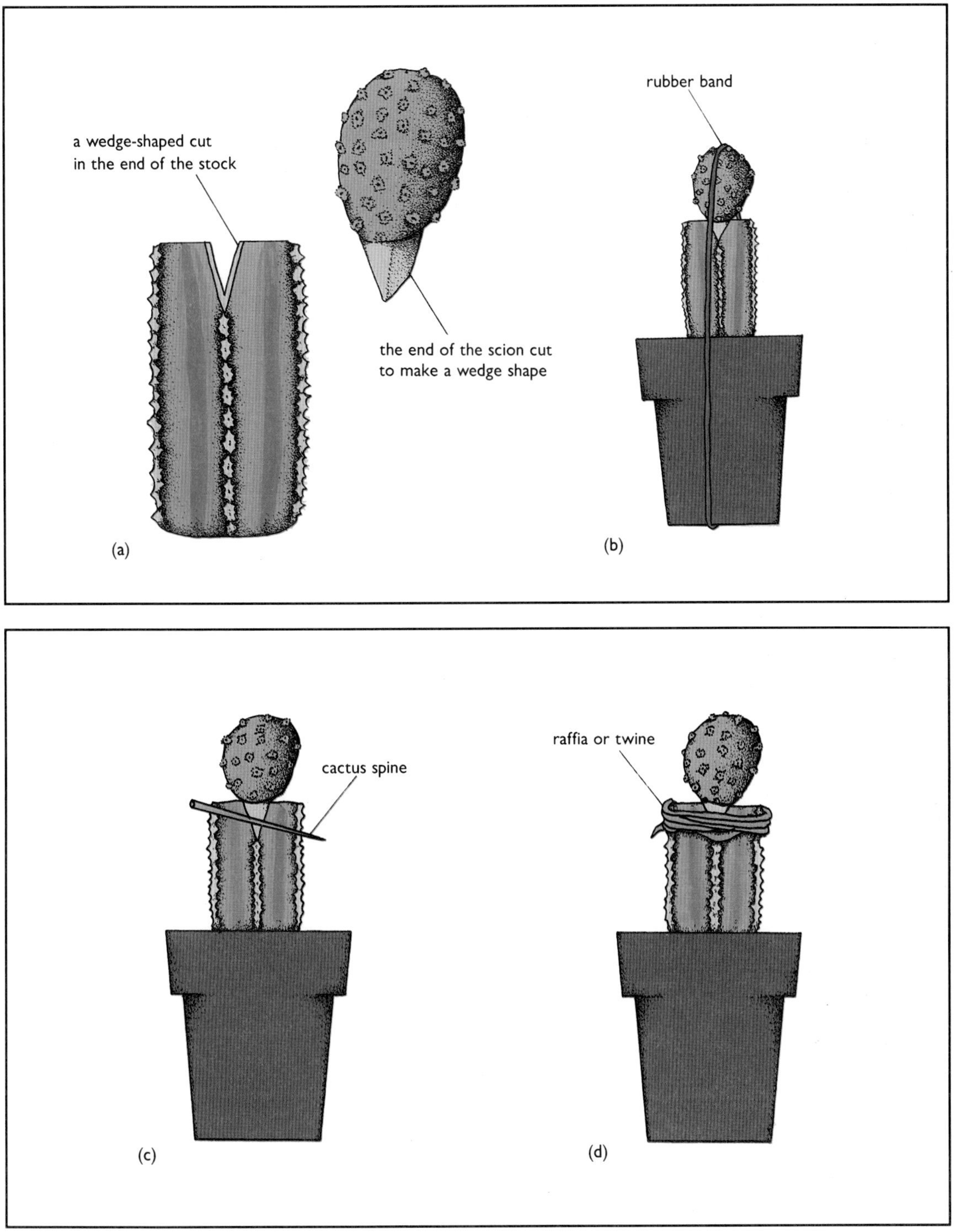

Fig 48 The cleft graft; (a) the stock and scion cut into an interlocking v-shape (b) the use of a rubber band to hold the graft (c) a cactus spine can also be used for this purpose (d) the third option is to use raffia of twine to bind the graft.

Fig 49 Mammillaria guelzowiana

distinguishable from the parent, and certainly of no more merit, occasionally an improved form is produced. It is the challenge of producing such improvements that attracts the hybridist, who will attempt to combine the best features of the two parents. Some succulent plant groups have been the subject of deliberate hybridisation for a very long time, so that today the hybrids are more widely grown than the species: this is particularly true of *Echeveria* and the epiphytic cacti.

Those who dabble in the art of plant breeding should have a definite aim. It is pointless to transfer pollen from plant to plant at random, in the vague hope that this will produce a worthwhile hybrid. The object should be to combine two desirable characteristics from the parents.

Some species are self-fertile, that is they set seed when pollen is transferred from the anthers to the stigma of the same flower. Others are self-sterile and must have pollen from another plant of the same species to produce true seed, or from a related species to produce hybrid seed. To ensure that the required hybridisation takes place, it is essential to prevent self-pollination or pollination by some other agency. To do this the hybridist carries out some delicate operations on the flower. As soon as it opens naturally, or just before, the stamens (which support the anthers) are removed, taking care to avoid damaging the stigma. This prevents self-pollination. The emasculated flower must then be protected from pollinating agents by enclosing it within an insect-proof shield. When the stigma is receptive, which occurs some time after the flower first opens, ripe pollen is transferred to it from the second parent. If pollination has been successful, a fruit containing viable seeds will eventually be produced.

It is very important to keep an adequate record of each crossing made. Memory is fickle, and if a worthwhile hybrid is obtained, its value is enhanced if its parentage is known. As it is likely that the seeds obtained from a single crossing will produce plants with different characteristics, it is desirable to grow them all on to flowering size to avoid missing the 'one in a million' outstanding hybrid.

CHAPTER 5

A Selection of Suitable Plants: Cacti

There are, in total, several thousand succulent plants, but no one would pretend that all are deserving of cultivation. Some are uninteresting weeds of no horticultural merit. Others, for example most species of *Sempervivum*, are attractive and worth cultivating, but as they are sufficiently hardy to be grown out-of-doors they are considered not to fall within the scope of this book. Among the plants that are both attractive and tender enough to need indoor protection during our winters, there are many that are not really suitable for an amateur's collection. These include the plants that grow too large or so rapidly as to become an embarrassment within a short time, and those that propagate so rapidly from seed or fallen leaves as to be regarded as invasive weeds. There are also plants that pose particular difficulties in cultivation. Although these include many beautiful plants, the novice is advised to delay their acquisition until experience has been gained by growing the easier kinds.

Even after eliminating a large number, there

Fig 50 Mammillaria zeilmanniana v. alba.

still remains an extensive range of plants worthy of cultivation. In a book of this size it is not possible to do more than scratch the surface. It would be superficial to attempt to include all the genera containing suitable plants, or all the species within the selected genera. Instead, a limited selection is offered which, it is hoped, will guide the novice towards the kinds of plant that will provide satisfaction.

The basis of selection embraces a number of factors:

1. The plants should be readily available from such sources as the specialist nursery. They include established favourites and recent discoveries that have been propagated in sufficient quantities to be offered for sale.

2. The plants should be suitable for indoor cultivation. For this reason many of the columnar cacti are omitted, as well as succulents that grow to tree-like proportions. A few exceptions are included: plants that grow slowly and are attractive as young plants, so are suitable for cultivation for a number of years before being discarded.

3. The plants should not pose particular difficulty in cultivation. This factor excludes some desirable plants that require temperatures higher than a winter minimum of about 40 °F (5 °C) such as *Melocactus*, *Discocactus* and *Pachypodium*. Also excluded are several 'tricky' plants for which higher temperatures are not the answer, such as *Sclerocactus* and some of the Stapeliads.

4. The plants should be attractive in appearance and preferably free-flowering while still small, though we have to accept that some plants are extremely unlikely to flower in cultivation in Europe yet are still worth growing.

The selection is a personal one, most of the plants mentioned having been grown by the author. Undoubtedly the reader will discover

Fig 51 Cotyledon galpinii.

other species in the same genera equally attractive. These are likely to be as suitable as those included – though there are the occasional 'difficult' species in many genera – and should not be discounted because they are not featured in the book.

For convenience, the cacti are described first, with the genera dealt with in alphabetical order. The other succulents follow in Chapter 6, the families and the genera within them being arranged alphabetically. Unfortunately, changing fashions in nomenclature have led to plants being classified and given names, then reclassified and renamed, sometimes several times. There is also a divergence of opinion between taxonomists who prefer a small number of large genera ('lumpers') and those who prefer a larger number of small genera ('splitters'). This has frequently led to the same plant being placed by different authorities (and even occasionally by the same authority!) in different genera and to its receiving several different names. In general a conservative approach, favouring the 'lumping' school, is adopted in this book, but where plants are more likely to be found under other names, attention is drawn to the fact.

CACTACEAE

The botanical Family Cactaceae contains a wide variety of forms, from tiny globular plants a few millimetres in diameter to columnar plants tens of metres tall. Between these extremes may be found cacti with spherical or cylindrical bodies 3ft (Im) or more in diameter, clumps of few or many heads, shrubby types, plants in which the stems are flattened, a few with slender climbing stems and others that hang orchid-like from tree branches. The one feature possessed by all and distinguishing them from other plants is the areole, which was described earlier in this book.

A question commonly posed by newcomers to the hobby concerns the number of species. Perhaps those who enquire have the intention of collecting them all. Unfortunately, it is not easy to answer the question with precision. It would be possible to count the number of validly published names, but there are in addition many that appear in nursery lists or in the literature that have not been formally published. Among the validly published names is a huge number that have been discarded as the result of reclassification. There is also the problem of synonymy, when the same plant has been described under more than one name. If further study leads to conviction that only one plant is involved, the name published first is retained and the later names discarded. During periods when 'lumping' is in fashion, the number of recognised types reduces, but when 'splitting' returns to favour, names proliferate. The number of published names runs to several thousands, but of these probably no more than two thousand would be recognised now by a supporter of the 'splitting' faction and many fewer by a conservative 'lumper'. It is almost as difficult to define the number of genera in the Family. A quarter of a century ago a leading authority produced a classification with over three hundred genera. A more modern treatment recognises fewer than a hundred genera. There will always be controversy between the proponents of the two schools, but this need not concern the novice.

Fig 52 Echinocereus reichenbachii v. baileyi.

Acanthocalycium

This genus of about a dozen species from Argentina has been included with both *Echinopsis* and *Lobivia*. In general, collectors do not seem to have favoured such moves and most continue to keep the genera separate. The feature distinguishing this genus from its relatives is the spiny bud which gives it its name.

The most commonly encountered species, and perhaps the most attractive, is *Acanthocalycium violaceum*. It grows fairly slowly to become a spherical to slightly cylindrical body 4–6in (10–15cm) in diameter. The body is ribbed, and armed with yellow to pale-brown curved spines. Flowers are produced in a ring close to the apex, and are trumpet-shaped, about 3in (75mm) long and, in a good form, of a delightful pale-lilac colour. The flowers are somewhat variable from one plant to another, sometimes being almost white, so it is advisable either to purchase a plant in flower or to grow several from seed to select a good form.

Aporocactus

This Mexican genus of epiphytic cacti contains only a few species (some would claim as few as two). Their attraction as flowering plants led to them being widely cultivated in their homeland, while elsewhere they have been crossed with other epiphytic cacti to produce some fine hybrids.

A. flagelliformis is commonly known as the 'Rat's Tail Cactus', an appellation deriving from the pendent habit of its slender stems. The stems are up to ¾in (2cm) in diameter and may grow to 3ft (1m) or more in length in favourable conditions. As offsets are produced from near the base of the stems, this is an ideal subject for a hanging basket, from which the stems cascade downwards. The armament comprises short, slender spines, yellow to pale brown in colour. The crowning glory of this plant is the multitude of bright-scarlet flowers produced along the stem and lasting for several days.

It should be remembered that this is an epiphytic plant and an adequate supply of water is required during the growing season. It is also advisable to feed the plant more generously than the desert cacti. Precautions should be taken against red spider mite: these pests are often attracted to the plant and can extensively damage the soft epidermis.

Astrophytum

This genus of Mexican cacti is deservedly popular with growers. Although the number of species is small, there is considerable variation that has led to the naming of several varieties and forms, and even within a single variety there is still enough variation to encourage collectors to grow more than one specimen. The plants are normally solitary, though branched plants do sometimes occur among batches of seedlings or as the result of injury to the growing point.

Fig 53 Astrophytum ornatum.

The largest-growing and most robust species is *Astrophytum ornatum*, which can reach 10ft (3m) in height, though such examples are rare in the wild and more so in cultivation, where a globular plant 18in (0.5m) in diameter would be outstanding. There are usually about eight prominent ribs, carrying widely spaced areoles that bear stout, straight spines. Small white or near-white flecks on the surface give the plant a distinctive appearance. The density of this covering varies; in *A. ornatum* fa. *mirbelii* the flecking tends to be dense, while in fa. *glabrescens* it is much more sparse. During the summer, and often late into the autumn, large, lemon-yellow flowers are produced from the areoles near the apex.

Astrophytum myriostigma is smaller and slower in growth, taking many years to reach maturity. It usually has five ribs, along the edges of which are situated the areoles, but these are normally devoid of spines. A form with only four ribs has been named *A. myriostigma* fa. *quadricostatum*, though with age this often develops a fifth rib. The body of this species too

Fig 54 Astrophytum myriostigma.

is usually covered with white flecks, which in some specimens is so densely packed as to give the impression that the plants have been carved from a piece of chalk. At the other extreme there are forms (*glabrum* and *nudum*) in which the flecking is absent.

Astrophytum capricorne is a strikingly attractive plant. It is somewhat smaller than the preceding species, cultivated plants rarely exceeding 6in (15cm) in height, and has about eight prominent ribs. Its spination is the most attractive in the genus. The flexible spines, which range in colour from pale yellow-brown to black, are flattened and papery. The large flower is also distinctive, having a vivid red throat contrasting with the bright yellow of the petals. There are several varieties, differing in some details, and a similar plant has been given the name *Astrophytum senile*.

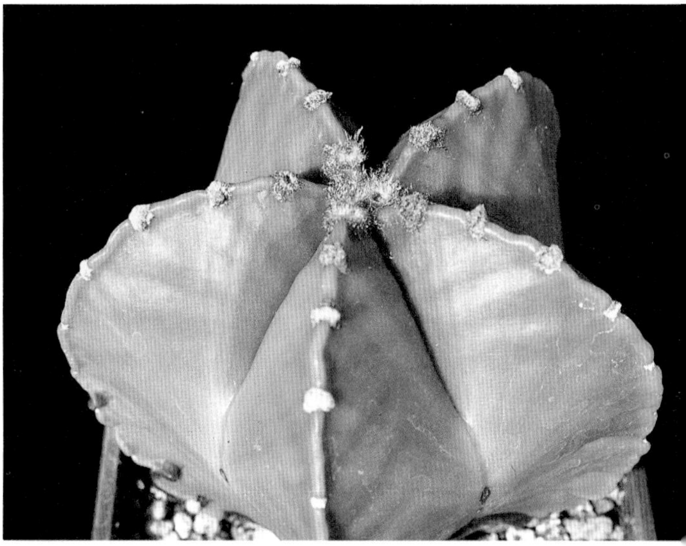

Fig 55 Astrophytum myriostigma f. glabrum.

Generally considered to be the aristocrat of the genus, *Astrophytum asterias* has a very different appearance from the others. The body is flattened, only about 1in (2.5cm) high and up to 4in (10cm) broad. The ribs are flat, scarcely detectable except by the lines of prominent areoles running along their centres. The flowers of this species too are yellow with a red throat.

Apart from *A. asterias*, the genus does not pose any particular difficulties. It is advisable not to pour water containing fertiliser over the bodies, or to spray with chemicals that might stain the flecking. As they age, the plants tend to become marked and woody around the base. This is a natural process and of no consequence unless the marking spreads too far up the sides of the plant. *A. asterias* is a little more temperamental and is best grown on a shelf in a very gritty compost and watered sparingly. Seedlings of this species tend to grow quite rapidly until about ½in (1cm) across, after which it is advisable to treat them more carefully, avoiding any temptation to hasten their growth.

Fig 56 Bolivicereus samaipatanus.

Bolivicereus

With this genus we reach our first tall-growing cactus and, simultaneously, the first major taxonomic problem!

In the 1960s a distinguished American botanist advanced convincing arguments in favour of transferring several genera of cacti into the genus *Borzicactus*. Among the plants are some with a columnar habit and others that are globular. Although his arguments found favour with other taxonomists, they have been slower in gaining acceptance among amateur growers. The result is that the same plant may be found labelled *Borzicactus* in a few collections and nurseries, but with some other name elsewhere. As it appears likely that growers will find the plants in nurseries or referred to in the literature under the original generic names, these will be used here.

Bolivicereus samaipatanus (*Borzicactus samaipatanus*) is a worthwhile addition to a collection on two counts. Firstly, it is an erect-growing plant, adding contrast of form to a display of predominantly globular plants. Secondly, it is a superb flowering plant, particularly as the appropriately named variety *multiflorus*. The stems are slender, about 1½in (3–4cm) in diameter but growing to over 3ft (1m) in length and tending to sprawl untidily unless trained up a support. Some prefer to grow it in a hanging basket, allowing the stems to hang down under their own weight. The bright-red flowers are produced along the stems, and when a large number open simultaneously the plant presents an unforgettable spectacle.

Carnegiea

Carnegiea gigantea is the giant saguaro, the branching columnar cactus so familiar to *aficionados* of the cowboy film. In the deserts of the American South West and across the border in Mexico, this is the most conspicuous cactus. Its fruit when, cooked, provides food for the Papago Indians of the area, while the fermented juice becomes an intoxicating drink. In the absence of trees, the trunk of the cactus is hollowed-out by woodpeckers who make their nests in the callus-lined holes.

In the wild, *C. gigantea* has a trunk 18in (0.5m) in diameter and grows to 40ft (12m). As such, it might not appear suitable for greenhouse cultivation, but growth is extremely slow. Even in the habitat, many years elapse before the plant attains sufficient height to begin branching. Thereafter, a few secondary stems appear and grow parallel to the main stem. It has been estimated that the largest specimens may be two centuries old. Cultivated plants grow just as slowly, and a 'seedling' 18in (0.5m) in height may be over thirty years old.

C. gigantea offers no difficulty in cultivation. It grows quite rapidly at first, but after the first year the rate decreases and it is often difficult to see much change in height from year to year. It slowly produces a massive stem, and is a worthwhile addition to a collection. The grower must, however, be resigned to the probability, nay certainty, that the plant will not flower in the greenhouse!

Cephalocereus

For most growers, the name *Cephalocereus* conjures up an image of the 'Old Man Cactus', *Cephalocereus senilis*. This is, however, a large genus, expanded considerably in recent years by the inclusion of a number of smaller genera. Even now, the number of species in general cultivation is small, despite the fact that many are very attractive.

C. senilis is an outstandingly attractive plant. Normally unbranched, it grows to a height of up to 50ft (15m) in the wild; in cultivation a plant 3ft (1m) in height would be a fine specimen. The stem is covered with long, white hair, particularly near the top, giving the plant a venerable appearance and the reason for its popular name. *C. senilis* is easily grown from seed into a handsome

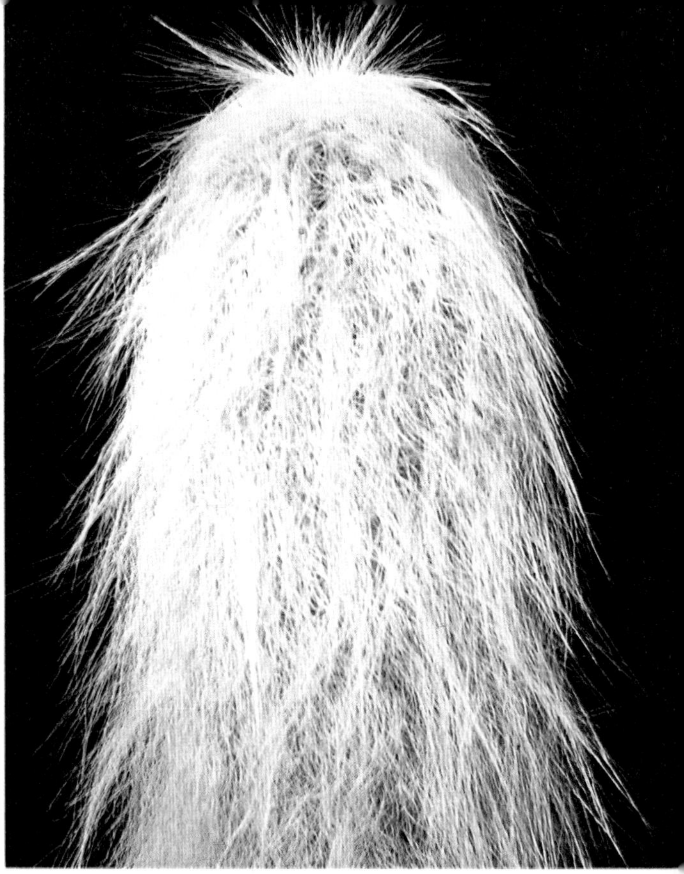

Fig 57 Cephalocereus senilis.

specimen provided a little care is taken. It should be grown in a gritty compost which must not be allowed to become too wet, otherwise there is a danger that the stem will rot at the base.

Cephalocereus palmeri may be found labelled *Pilosocereus palmeri*, having been transferred to and from the latter genus since its discovery in the early years of this century. The stem is dark bluish-green, with about eight prominent ribs carrying closely spaced areoles. As the plant matures, dense white wool is produced from near the top of the stem. It is from this wool that the large, short-tubed flowers originate. The flowers are pink and may appear on plants no more than 3ft (1m) tall.

Cephalocereus polylophus is likely to be found labelled with another name: *Neobuxbaumia polylophus*. It contrasts well with the preceding species, having a stout stem with fifteen to eighteen ribs carrying slender spines but no hair. Young seedlings have a neat appearance, and this persists as the plants mature.

Cleistocactus

This South American genus of fifty to sixty species includes some plants with relatively stout stems and fine spination that would earn a place in any collection, whether or not they flowered easily, and others of a more slender habit and sparser spination which nevertheless attract attention by their spectacular flowering performance.

The best-known species, *Cleistocactus strausii*, is an old favourite and deservedly so. It grows easily and steadily to form an upright stem about 2in (5cm) in diameter and 3ft (1m) or more in height. Often branching from the base, the stems are covered with slender, white, bristle-like spines. The attraction of the plant is further enhanced when flowers are produced, usually after the plant has reached a height of 18in (0.5m) or so. The flowers, about 3in (8cm) long and deep red in colour, appear from near the top of the stem.

Cleistocactus vulpis-cauda is a complete contrast. The species name means 'fox-tail', which aptly describes the appearance of the pendent stems, clad with fine spines which may vary from yellow to brown in colour. The flowers are bright red. Although this species is more difficult to accommodate than the upright types, it is worth making space for, perhaps in a hanging basket.

For further contrast, this time in flower colour, it is worth looking out for *Cleistocactus ritteri*, with yellow flowers. The slender-stemmed, less densely spined species should not be overlooked either. Some have brilliantly coloured flowers that are freely produced over a long period. Among these *Cleistocactus baumannii*, the first species to be discovered, can be recommended.

Cleistocacti are not difficult plants to grow, but they occasionally give cause for concern. Sometimes, for no discernible reason, a stem ceases to grow. It does not die back, but remains dormant. Occasionally, after a rest of several years, it will start to grow again. It is possible that if the plant has not been repotted for some time it may have exhausted some element in the compost, as repotting the plant sometimes jolts it into growth again.

Copiapoa

The genus receives its name from Copiapo in northern Chile, all the species being confined to that country between the Andes and the Pacific Ocean. There are two distinct groups of species. One group comprises the species that remain solitary or form small clumps of a few large bodies, while the other group contains species with smaller bodies, generally clustering to form large clumps and flowering freely while still young.

One of the most beautiful is *Copiapoa krainziana*. It is somewhat intermediate in size between the two groups defined above, having bodies 4–6in (10–15cm) in diameter but often offsetting freely to form clusters 3ft (1m) across. It is quite variable, a good form having a greyish body and long glassy-white spines. In other forms the spines may be brownish in colour.

Among the small-bodied species there are several worthy of a place. Although they are less strikingly attractive than *C. krainziana*, they are more easily obtained and are free-flowering. *Copiapoa humilis* has dark bodies, usually purplish but sometimes almost black. This plant proliferates by offsets produced at ground level, and soon becomes a solid clump of heads. *Copiapoa montana* is another dark-bodied plant, but with larger heads and offsetting less freely. *Copiapoa hypogea* has a large, turnip-like root and usually remains solitary. Unlike *C. krainziana*, all of these species can be relied upon to flower, producing yellow blooms from the apex.

The group of larger-bodied species tend to remain solitary for much longer, though most offset eventually to form clumps of a few heads. In the extreme conditions of their habitat, the plants grow slowly into eye-catching specimens. The mature bodies are spherical to short-cylindrical, and in most of the species they are chalky-white in colour, contrasting with stout, black spines. Seedlings are initially green or olive-green, but if

Fig 58 Copiapoa tenuissima.

they are grown slowly they gradually develop a whitish coloration, though this is never so pronounced as in the habitat.

Copiapoa cinerea is one of the most attractive. Although slow, it is not difficult to grow and with its stout, black spines it is handsome at all stages. *Copiapoa haseltoniana*, considered by some to be a variety of this species (*C. cinerea* var. *haseltoniana*) is another attractive plant with an olive-green body and yellow spines.

From their generally sturdy appearance, and with a knowledge of the climatic conditions in their habitat, it might be supposed that Copiapoas offer no problems in cultivation. There are two areas where a little caution is advisable however. If the plants are over-watered, particularly in the early part of the year, it is possible to split the skin which, though not fatal, can leave unsightly scars. There is another danger if plants are exposed to strong sunlight, as the bodies are easily scorched.

Coryphantha

This large genus of about eighty species has an undeserved reputation for being difficult to flower. It is true that some of the larger-growing types need to be mature before they begin to bloom, but others flower as small plants. The flowers, predominantly yellow, are large and showy so every gardener will find that success with these plants is satisfying.

The distribution extends from the Canadian provinces of British Columbia and Alberta to southern Mexico. The variation in the plants is considerable, and some of the smaller species have been transferred to *Escobaria*, though they will still be discovered labelled *Coryphantha*. Some types remain solitary, growing slowly to produce globular bodies; others produce cylindrical stems which become top-heavy and sprawl over the ground. Some begin to offset while still young, quickly developing into large mounds.

Fig 59 Coryphantha pallida.

Coryphantha bumamma is a clustering plant with large, rounded tubercles carrying recurving, yellowish-brown spines. This species always seems to have a healthy glow, which is enhanced when the large, yellow flowers are produced from the apex. *Coryphantha elephantidens* is a plant of similar appearance, but with distinctive pink flowers.

Among the species that can be relied upon to flower at a relatively small size, *Coryphantha pallida* has a globular body, with bluish-green tubercles tipped with a cluster of white spines, and white hair in the apex. The flowers are large and very pale yellow to white.

Although most species pose no difficulty in cultivation, some are prone to an affliction which spoils their appearance. Many of the species possess nectary glands on the stem which exude a sticky secretion. If not removed, this tends to develop a sooty black mould which, while apparently harmless, is unsightly. If you want to prevent the fungus from becoming established, it is advisable to spray the plants from time to time with warm water containing a fungicide.

Echinocactus

The outstanding species in this genus is undoubtedly the 'Golden Barrel Cactus', *Echinocactus grusonii*, sometimes maliciously named 'Mother-in-law's Chair'. It would be difficult to conceive a more uncomfortable seat since this plant forms a large, spherical body armed with stout spines up to 2in (5cm) long.

E. grusonii is an interesting plant to grow from seed. At first the body has tubercles carrying the areoles at their tips; later the tubercles unite to form prominent ribs. The plant normally remains solitary until of considerable size, though multi-headed specimens occur occasionally among batches of seedlings. Once the body has reached the size of a football, this is a handsome specimen indeed. The spination is yellow, sometimes pale almost to the point of being described as white and sometimes a deep golden colour. It is densest at the top of the plant, which also becomes woolly with age.

This is a robust plant, but worth protecting from exposure to cold as this can cause marking of the body. It cannot be pretended that it is easily flowered, though some growers have succeeded. Flowering performance seems to be related to size or age, and the plants that have flowered in cultivation have been large ones.

Echinocereus

This genus of nearly fifty species occurs in Mexico and south-west USA. It is admirably suited to cultivation since the majority of species are undemanding with regard to temperature and reliable in their flowering performance.

There is considerable variation in the appearance of the plants. The stems may be solitary or clustering, globular, cylindrical or elongated. The spination may be short and slender, hairlike or absent. The flowers are equally variable, ranging from the small, yellowish-green blooms of *Echinocereus viridiflorus* to the large, brilliantly coloured flowers of *Echinocereus pectinatus* and *Echinocereus pentalophus*.

Fig 60 Echinocereus viridiflorus v. davisii.

In the main, Echinocerei are robust plants and will survive low temperatures. Some growers even go so far as to overwinter the plants in an unheated frame or greenhouse, claiming that this apparently harsh treatment encourages them to flower profusely. It is perhaps safer to maintain a temperature just above freezing point during the winter – plants seem to flower just as freely. Most species require an adequate supply of water during the warmer months, but the compost should be allowed to dry out during the autumn and winter. This is particularly important in the case of species with tuberous roots, such as *Echinocereus pulchellus*.

Red spider mite can sometimes be a problem. The pests seem to be attracted to the soft-bodied types such as *Echinocereus knippelianus*, and the scars resulting from such attacks will remain visible for a long time.

The novice grower is often alarmed to see a small bulge on a stem, which splits to allow the emergence of an offset or flower-bud. This is natural behaviour in some species and, although

Fig 61 Echinocereus pulchellus.

a minor irritant, the resulting scar should be accepted with equanimity: there is nothing the grower can do to prevent it! Flowering also tends to leave a permanent scar in some species. If flowers are produced late in the year, there is always a danger that the open wounds left when they drop will be susceptible to fungal attack. Dusting the wounds with green sulphur should prevent this.

It would be difficult to mention a species that is *not* worth growing, but for the purposes of this book it will suffice to describe a handful as the basis of a collection. The reader is encouraged to try others that catch the eye.

Among the species with slender stems, *E. pentalophus* is strongly recommended. It was first collected in the early nineteenth century, and has remained a firm favourite ever since. The plant clusters freely, the branches tending to remain prostrate. The stems are slender and soft in texture and care is needed when handling the plants to avoid breaking off areoles and spine clusters.

Fig 62 Echinocereus scheeri.

Flowers are produced freely, even on small plants, and open to 5in (12cm) or more in diameter. The pinkish-magenta of the outer part is balanced by the cream of the innermost parts, and the surface of the flower has a glossy sheen.

Echinocereus scheeri is another slender-stemmed species, but in this case the stems are stiffer. Its flower may be pink, red or orange, the latter often being offered for sale under the name *Echinocereus salm-dyckianus*. There is also the interesting variety *gentryi*, which is almost spineless.

Echinocereus triglochidiatus and its several varieties are worth growing, though it may be some years before the strikingly attractive flowers are produced. It is not difficult to grow, though sometimes rather slow, but it is somewhat reluctant to flower until fully mature. The flowers are worth waiting for: long-tubed and brilliant orange-red, they are thought to be pollinated by hummingbirds in the habitat.

Many of the Echinocerei have dense attractive spination of sufficient merit to ensure the plants' popularity even if they did not flower. When the flowers are also large and colourful, the appeal is complete. *Echinocereus rigidissimus* is one such beauty. The stem is usually solitary, short-cylindrical and densely covered by the spines. The latter are produced from long narrow areoles, in comb-like arrangements which interlace to conceal the body completely. The spines vary in colour, producing a banded appearance which led to the plant being given the popular name 'Rainbow Cactus'. The flowers are striking, having a white throat and purplish-pink outer petals. The plant was at one time considered to be a variety of *E. pectinatus* and may still be found labelled *E. pectinatus* var. *rigidissimus*.

Another species with elongated areoles and pectinate (comb-like) spine clusters is *Echinocereus reichenbachii*. Seedling plants 2in (5cm) or so tall are usually available and are always eye-catching. They often begin to flower at this size, though eventually they may grow to 12in (30cm) in height, with a few stout branches. The flowers are among the most attractive in the genus, being dusky pink set off by a darker throat filled with golden stamens.

Echinocereus subinermis is likely to be mistaken for an Echinopsis when not in flower, even by experienced growers. The body is globular with clearly defined ribs and small areoles. Some forms of the plant are spineless, while others produce a few weak spines. This species is notable for its tubular, bright-yellow flowers.

Superficially similar, though on a smaller scale, *E. knippelianus* multiplies to form a flat mound of bodies with tuberous rootstocks. This species too may be spineless or possess a few slender spines. The flowers, produced early in the year, are small and pink.

A species that is worth seeking, though it is not easy to find, is *Echinocereus delaetii*. The beauty of this plant lies in the long, white hairs clothing the semi-prostrate stems. Unfortunately it is shy-flowering, but this should not deter since the plant is outstandingly attractive even without flowers.

Echinopsis

Until comparatively recent times, the South American genus *Echinopsis*, at least as found in cultivation, was clearly delimited. Most collections contained a few examples, superficially similar in appearance and notable mainly for their large, trumpet-shaped and sweetly scented flowers in white or pale pink, which open in the late afternoon and wilt during the next day. Complications began with the expansion of the genus to include a number of species which some would place in a separate genus *Pseudolobivia*. These are generally smaller plants, producing white, yellow or pink flowers which open during the day rather than at night. More recently, the genus has been expanded further to include *Trichocereus* (and several other small and rarely grown genera of columnar plants). This merger has met with greater resistance from collectors, though the arguments in favour appear to be well founded. In this book *Trichocereus* is treated as a separate genus.

Of the 'traditional' species, *Echinopsis eyriesii* is both the most common and the best. It has dark-green, globular bodies, prominently ribbed, and offsets to form large mounds. The areoles are widely spaced on the angles of the ribs, and from these are produced spines about 0.2in (5mm) long. The nocturnal flowers are produced from the areoles in the upper part of the stem. They are tubular, up to 10in (25cm) long, white and sweet-scented.

Among the Pseudolobivias there are several distinctive plants that are worthy of collection. *Echinopsis (Pseudolobivia) ferox* lives up to its species name, which means 'fierce'. The central spines are up to 6in (15cm) long and curve in such a way as to entangle themselves with anything that approaches them too closely. This species has long-tubed, white flowers.

Echinopsis (Pseudolobivia) kermesina has more modest armament, straight, slender spines about ½in (1cm) long, but a more spectacular flower. The true species has carmine flowers up

Fig 63 Echinopsis kermesina.

to 6in (15cm) or so in length, but there are many imposters which have paler pink flowers.

Another very attractive species, requiring considerably less space, is *Echinopsis (Pseudolobivia) carmineoflora*. This has a slightly flattened globular body, up to 3in (7cm) in diameter and 1½in (4cm) tall. The flowers vary (on different plants) from carmine to a paler salmon or flesh colour.

Mention should be made of the range of attractive hybrids that have been produced by crossing *Echinopsis* with *Lobivia*. The resulting offspring have tended to inherit the body form of *Echinopsis*, but have benefited from the introduction of colour from the *Lobivia* parent. Although purists may dismiss these hybrids, other growers welcome the enhanced colour range and free-flowering habit of the plants.

Epithelantha

Although a number of plants of differing appearance have been given species names, it is more sensible to treat this as a monotypic genus with the single species *Epithelantha micromeris* and several varieties. Years ago mature clumps were collected from the habitats in Texas and northern Mexico and were offered to growers who regarded them highly. This despoiling of the habitat, together with other factors, led to the wild populations being reduced to the point where the plant was placed on the list of endangered species. Fortunately the plants are easily raised from seed, and today it is possible to purchase young specimens at modest prices from the specialist nurseries.

E. micromeris is a small and slow-growing cactus. The body is globular, up to 1½in (4cm) in diameter, sometimes remaining solitary but often offsetting to form a small clump. It is densely covered with short, white spines and often produces a quantity of short wool at the apex. The small flowers, pale pink in colour, appear from the crown, often followed by bright-red fruits.

It is advisable to grow *E. micromeris* in a gritty compost and to water it sparingly. A position on a shelf close to the glass, where it will receive maximum light, suits it very well.

Fig 64 Epithelantha micromeris.

Escobaria

This small genus of attractive cacti has been expanded in recent years to include several plants that were previously placed in other genera, and are generally better known under the original names. The group shows considerable diversity, from species with small, tightly spined bodies to others with larger bodies and a more open habit and a few which eventually form large clumps.

The Mexican *Escobaria roseana*, sometimes found labelled *Gymnocactus roseanus*, is one of the clustering species with individual bodies about 1½in (4cm) in diameter. The interlacing, slender spines are yellow and the flowers are yellow with a darker midstripe.

Escobaria dasyacantha, from the other side of the United States/Mexico border, has a cylindrical body densely covered with slender, white spines. It usually remains solitary, but may produce a few offsets. The flowers, produced from the stem apex, are pale pink.

Escobaria missouriensis, perhaps better known as *Neobesseya missouriensis*, does not receive its name from the state of Missouri but from the river flowing through its habitat in the

Fig 65 Escobaria dasyacantha.

Fig 66 Escobaria minima.

Great Plains area of the northern United States. This plant has a rather open habit, which becomes more pronounced when it takes up water during the period of active growth. The flowers, about lin (2.5cm) in diameter, are yellowish in colour.

The gem of the genus is *Escobaria minima*, which has also received the name *Escobaria nellieae* as well as being placed in *Coryphantha* with the same species names. *E. minima* is tiny, with cylindrical stems no more than lin (2.5cm) in diameter. Sometimes the plant remains solitary, but more frequently it branches to form a small cluster. The stems are completely hidden by the dense spination radiating from large areoles. The spines are cream, often tipped with pink (especially while young), and deep-pinkish-purple flowers are freely produced from the stem apex.

In general the Escobarias require a little extra caution when watering. It is advisable to use a very well-drained compost and to position the plants on a shelf in full sun.

Espostoa

Espostoas are among the most handsome of the columnar cacti. In cultivation they are usually seen as single stems, reaching 3ft (lm) or more, though in the wild they grow to the proportions of small trees. The appearance of the plants is rather deceptive. The stems are densely covered with white hairs, which often conceal the primary armament of sharp spines. The unwary admirer stroking the stem may have a surprise!

Espostoa lanata, from northern Peru, has red-tipped central spines which protrude through the hair to give the plants a pinkish tinge. The variety *sericata* lacks these central spines.

The species from central Peru, which are sometimes placed in a separate genus *Pseudoespostoa*, are somewhat smaller in stature and more densely covered with wool. *Espostoa melanostele* has stout stems, occasionally branching from the base. As it matures, this species often produces long, yellow central spines. *Espostoa nana* is similar but somewhat smaller. In both species the wool at the apex forms a dense mass like cotton-wool.

The genus *Thrixanthocereus*, with three species, is often included in *Espostoa*. The most attractive species is *Espostoa (Thrixanthocereus) senilis*, which often branches from near the base to form a group of slender stems clad with white spines and hairs.

It is a rare occurrence, though not unknown, for these plants to flower in the greenhouse. The first indication is the development of the cephalium from which the flowers are produced. The cephalium is an area of wool or bristles on the side of the stem which, for those fortunate enough to observe it, may be thought to be some kind of malformed growth.

Espostoas are sometimes considered to be a little more tender than most cacti, but the author's experience does not support that view. Over a period of many years the plants have come to no harm in a greenhouse where the winter temperature often approaches freezing point. It is advisable, however, to keep the compost dry during the colder part of the year.

Ferocactus

The genus *Ferocactus*, native to Mexico and the south-western USA, contains some of the large-growing 'barrel cacti' which, were they to grow to full size in cultivation, would be too large for most of us to accommodate. This, however, takes many years and so does not present any problem. Many species are very attractive as young plants and can be enjoyed until they become an embarrassment, while a few are fully mature and will flower at a small size.

Among the smaller species, *Ferocactus fordii*

Fig 67 Ferocactus acanthodes.

and *Ferocactus viridescens* are excellent plants for those with limited space. Both species will flower in small pots. *F. fordii* has a flattened globular stem with acute ribs. One central spine is larger than the others, has a hooked tip and is directed downwards. The plant will produce its purplish-pink flowers when no more than 4in (10cm) in diameter. *F. viridescens* possesses downward-directed, hooked central spines which are red or yellow. The flowers, produced from the crown of the plant, are yellowish-green.

Ferocactus glaucescens grows to a diameter of 20–25in (50–60cm), albeit slowly. It is a striking plant with a blue-green epidermis and straight yellow spines. Flowering specimens are occasionally seen, but it seems that the plant needs to be 6–8in (15–20cm) in diameter before the yellow flowers are produced.

Another species much appreciated by collectors is *Ferocactus latispinus*. This has a flattened globular body, prominent ribs and large areoles from which the spines appear. The outstanding feature of this species is the cluster of four central spines. All are stout and transversely ridged, but the lower one is very broad and recurved, making it a formidable weapon. The spines are red, and this colour (as in the other species) is enhanced when the plants are sprayed.

A small-growing and free-flowering plant, still more frequently known as *Hamatocactus setispinus*, has recently been transferred to become *Ferocactus setispinus*. It grows to about 4in (10cm) in diameter, with irregular ribs and slender spines, the central one being sharply hooked. Large, yellow flowers with red throats are produced from the top of the plant. It is a prolific and reliable performer.

Ferocacti are undemanding plants, requiring no more than a reasonably porous compost, adequate water and plenty of sunshine. Some do, however, pose a problem. They have glands in the areoles which exude a sticky secretion, and if left on the plants this encourages the growth of a sooty mould. It can be discouraged by spraying with warm water at frequent intervals.

Gymnocalycium

This large South American genus, with close to a hundred species, is characterised by the lack of hair or spines on the flower-tube indicated by its name, meaning 'naked bud'. There is a general similarity, in that the plant bodies are globular or flattened, but a sufficient diversity of size, spination and flower colour to enthuse collectors.

In general the plants are not difficult to cultivate, but since their distribution range is a large one, covering in excess of twenty degrees of latitude, their geographical origins should be taken into account. Those species from the northern end of the range, from Paraguay and southern Bolivia, appreciate warmer conditions, while those from the southern extremity of the range in Patagonia will withstand much cooler conditions. Many are plants of the Argentinian

Fig 68 Gymnocalycium bruchii.

grasslands and are somewhat sensitive to strong sunshine even in the European climate. It is advisable to provide protection against scorching, either by positioning them in the shade of other plants or even by growing them under the staging of glass-to-ground greenhouses.

With such a wide choice of species, it is possible only to proffer a few personal favourites and leave the reader to discover the delights of other species. It is unlikely that any will disappoint.

Gymnocalycium bruchii is a popular species. It has small bodies and offsets prolifically to form large flat clusters. The spines are white, sometimes projecting and sometimes closely following the body contour. The plant flowers very freely, producing masses of pretty pink flowers early in the year.

Sturdy spination always attracts interest, and that of *Gymnocalycium pungens* is eye-catching. The plant body reaches about 3in (8cm) in diameter with irregular, humped ribs and large areoles, from which 1½in (4cm) straight spines project outwards. It presents a ferocious appearance, relieved by the production of white flowers.

Gymnocalycium horridispinum is another strongly spined species. Unlike most members of the genus, this one tends to grow columnar with its straight spines projecting outwards. The flowers are usually bright pink, though forms with paler flowers have been reported.

Red flowers are uncommon in this genus, so *Gymnocalycium baldianum* (sometimes labelled *Gymnocalycium venturianum*) is worthy of inclusion. The body, blue-grey in colour, may reach 3in (8cm) in diameter. The flowers, like those of most members of the genus, are produced from areoles near the apex of the stem. In this species they are deep red.

As a contrast in flower colour, *Gymnocalycium andreae* can be recommended. This is a clustering species with individual bodies about 2in (5cm) in diameter. The spines are weak, but the flowers are a rich sulphur-yellow.

Gymnocalycium denudatum is a variable species and a number of varietal names have been generated for what are really no more than geographical forms. The distinctive feature, which attracts the attention at once, is the cluster of slender spines which recurve to lie close to the body. The cluster has an uncanny resemblance to a spider and has given rise to the popular name 'Spider Cactus'. The long-tubed flowers, white or pale pink, reach nearly 3in (7cm) in diameter.

One of the prettiest species is *Gymnocalycium friedrichii*, sometimes regarded as a variety of *Gymnocalycium mihanovichii*. The body has sharply angular ribs and is attractively marked with a pattern of parallel bands. The pink flowers are freely produced, even on very young plants. This species comes from Paraguay, and in common with other species from that area appreciates warmer growing conditions.

Not all Gymnocalyciums are small, and among the larger-growing species *Gymnocalycium saglione* is outstanding. It normally remains solitary, slowly growing to 12in (30cm) or so. As a young plant it is very attractive, with ribs divided into large tubercles and strong curving spines, and its attractions increase with maturity. The plant usually has to be of a reasonable size, say 4in (10cm) in diameter, before the short-tubed, white flowers are produced.

Haageocereus

The members of this Peruvian genus are not as widely grown as they deserve to be, and this neglect can be attributed to the demands they eventually make on space. With a few exceptions, young plants are columnar, but with age they tend to branch from the base and often sprawl across their neighbours.

The main attraction lies in the handsome spination, which ranges from near-white through shades of yellow and brown to almost black. Generally the plants have to be several years old before they can be expected to flower, though small plants of *Haageocereus decumbens* may produce white flowers with brownish outer petals, opening in late afternoon and remaining open through the night. It is worth persevering

Fig 69 Hildewintera aureispina.

with a few of the species though, as their flowers are large and often colourful.

With somewhere in the region of forty species to select from, most of which are quite variable in the colour of their spination, it is likely that the hobbyist will select plants with 'eye-appeal'. Among these, *Haageocereus chosicensis* and *Haageocereus versicolor*, which has several varieties with different spination, can be recommended.

Plants are easily raised from seed and quickly develop into attractive specimens. They are a little more sensitive to cold than most of the columnar cacti mentioned in this work, and should be given a warm and sunny position.

Hildewintera

This plant was first described as *Winteria aureispina*, the only member of a monotypic genus, but has since suffered several changes of name. The generic name has been changed to *Winterocereus*, *Loxanthocereus* and *Hildewintera*, and there has been an atempt to submerge it in the catch-all *Borzicactus*, but the plant appears to be most frequently encountered with the label *Hildewintera aureispina*.

It is a beautiful plant, though its branching pendent habit makes it difficult to accommodate, except in a hanging basket. The stems, about lin (2.5cm) in diameter, may reach 3ft (lm) or more in length. They are densely covered with golden-yellow spines which are deceptively sharp and likely to surprise the unwary admirer tempted to run a hand along the stem. The tubular flowers, about 2in (5cm) long and broad, are produced along the stems. Their colour is difficult to describe, somewhere between salmon-pink and orange. Often the plant flowers several times in a season.

This is a superb flowering plant when it can be given sufficient space to develop. It offers no difficulty in cultivation, but if grown in a hanging basket it will need plenty of water during hot weather.

Leuchtenbergia

Leuchtenbergia is a monotypic genus, containing the single species *Leuchtenbergia principis*. In general appearance this plant must be ranked among the most unusual in the Cactaceae. The body comprises a number of long tubercles, triangular in cross-section, arising from a tuberous rootstock. Each tubercle carries an areole at its tip, from which long, papery spines are produced. The yellow flowers, satiny in texture, are produced from areoles near the growing point.

Perhaps because of its bizarre appearance, and also the fact that it was discovered in a very arid mountain area of Coahuila, Mexico, a certain mystique has attached to this plant and its cultivation. Recommendations have been made that the plant should be watered very sparingly and infrequently, but such extreme caution is quite unnecessary. Certainly, as with all tuberous-rooted cacti, it is advisable to use a well-drained potting compost, but the plant needs an adequate supply of water during the growing period.

Plants usually become rather scruffy in appearance as the papery spines are fragile and are easily broken or detached. The older tubercles tend to lose their spines completely and gradually wither away. In consequence, the lower part of the body of a mature plant presents a battered appearance. This is completely natural, however, and not an indication that the cultural regime is at fault.

Lobivia

For some reason, *Lobivia* does not enjoy the popularity it deserves. None of the species

Fig 70 Leuchtenbergia principis.

grows too large to be accommodated in a small collection: those that offset prolifically to produce large clumps can be broken up from time to time. The majority flower freely, and the range of flower colour is second to none in the Family. Perhaps it is the short life of individual flowers, usually only a day or so, that is responsible for the apparent neglect, but in compensation many species flower several times in a season.

Lobivia is a genus of the Andean chain, the distribution range extending from southern Peru, through south-western Bolivia and into north-western Argentina. The plants are undemanding in cultivation, requiring only a well-lit situation with ample water in summer, and will withstand temperatures approaching freezing point. They are easily raised from seed and will often begin to flower when three or four years old. The freely clustering species often produce offsets which root down alongside the parent. These offsets may be detached complete with their root systems and be potted up directly, thus making propagation extremely easy.

Fig 71 Lobivia backebergii ssp. schieliana.

Fig 72 Lobivia backebergii ssp. wrightiana v. winteriana.

The species most widely cultivated is undoubtedly *Lobivia silvestrii*, better known under the name *Chamaecereus silvestrii*. This is ideally suited to windowsill culture, where it grows happily and smothers itself with vivid orange-red flowers. The finger-like stems are clothed with tiny soft spines, which enhance its appeal as a houseplant. The merits of this species have led to its selection as parent of a range of hybrids. These usually have stouter and stiffer stems and stronger spination, but retain the free-flowering characteristics of *L. silvestrii*. The range of flower colours available embraces yellow, orange, red and purple.

Many Lobivias occur over a large area and have diversified into a multiplicity of forms with varying spination and flower colour. Some of the more distinctive forms have received species names, but intensive study of the natural variation in recent years has led to many of these being reduced to subspecies or varieties. A typical example of a variable species is *Lobivia backebergii*, generally applied in cultivation to a small-bodied plant with bright-red flowers. The subspecies *schieliana*, formerly *Lobivia schieliana*, is a more columnar form with larger and paler flowers. The former *Lobivia wrightiana*, now *L. backebergii* ssp. *wrightiana*, offsets more sparingly and has long, twisted spines. Its flowers have long, slender tubes and are a delightful pale lilac-pink. In contrast, *L. backebergii* ssp. *wrightiana* var. *winteriana* (*Lobivia winteriana*) produces shorter spines and large, magenta flowers.

Fig 73 Lobivia aurea.

The flowers of the group of plants that have been reduced to varieties and forms of *Lobivia chrysantha* are the most beautiful in the genus. This group includes, among others, *Lobivia haageana*, *Lobivia cinnabarina*, *Lobivia jajoiana* and *Lobivia vatteri*. The flowers range from yellow through orange to shades of red, and are distinguished by a dark throat and prominent golden anthers.

Lobivia aurea may also be found labelled *Echinopsis aurea* or *Pseudolobivia aurea*. This is a small plant, usually remaining solitary, bearing a marked resemblance to an Echinopsis. Its tubular flowers are up to 3½in (9cm) in length and bright yellow.

Lophophora

This small genus occurs over a region from central Mexico northwards into Texas. Although there is little variation in the general appearance of the plants, several variants have been given names. Today it is generally considered that the genus contains but one species, *Lophophora williamsii*, or at most two, *L. williamsii* and *Lophophora diffusa*.

The plants are distinctive, having a stout, tuberous rootstock and a soft, flattened globular body, blue-green in colour. They are spineless, except as tiny seedlings when they possess short, soft spines. With maturity the spination is replaced by tufts of white or yellowish woolly felt, especially at the crown. The flowers range from pale yellow (sometimes labelled *Lophophora lutea*) to deep purplish-pink (*Lophophora jour-*

daniana), but are most commonly a delicate pale pink.

In the days when cacti were collected in great numbers from the wild for sale to collectors, *L. williamsii* was regarded with considerable awe. There is no justification for this however. Plants are easily raised from seed and grow quite quickly, often beginning to flower when less than lin (2.5cm) in diameter. Despite their tender appearance, the plants are tough, withstanding temperatures close to freezing point. A gritty compost is advisable, in keeping with the tuberous rootstock. Overhead watering and spraying of mature plants should be avoided: it will not necessarily harm the plant, but it causes the felt to mat together, thus spoiling the appearance of the plant.

Mamillopsis

This monotypic genus (unless one accepts the validity of a second and very similar species, *Mamillopsis diguetii*) provides employment for taxonomists. To the casual eye, *Mamillopsis senilis* has an obvious affinity with hook-spined members of the genus *Mammillaria*, but one school of thought considers the distinctive long-tubed, bright-red flowers sufficient to justify the genus *Mamillopsis*. An opposing school points to other species of *Mammillaria* with equally distinctive flowers and insists that *Mammillaria senilis* is a more appropriate name. At present it is likely that the plant will be offered for sale labelled *Mamillopsis senilis*.

M. senilis is an attractive clump-forming species, with bodies densely covered with white spines, one or more of the central spines being sharply hooked. The showy flowers, making a fine contrast with the spines, are produced from near the top of the plant. Flowering, however, is somewhat unpredictable. Sometimes young plants flower well for a year or two, but then cease blooming. Many theories have been advanced to explain this phenomenon. One is that the plants stop flowering when they start to offset. Another is that they require intense light to flower. A third explanation hinges on the origin of the plants in the mountains of Durango and Chihuahua, Mexico, where they are covered in snow during the winter.

This plant should be provided with a gritty compost and requires a little extra care when watering. It might be interesting to experiment with a group of seedlings, providing them with different growing conditions with the aim of persuading them to flower consistently.

Mammillaria

There is no doubt that, of all the genera of the Cactaceae, *Mammillaria* offers the greatest appeal to collectors. A large genus, with over two hundred species, it contains many plants that instantly attract, are easily and rapidly grown into large specimens, and reward the grower with a multiplicity of colourful flowers. For more experienced collectors there are choicer species, usually more difficult to grow but often with larger and more showy flowers. There are also a few that offer a real challenge and so, perversely, become even more desirable to enthusiasts.

As is usually the case with large genera having a wide distribution, in this case encompassing the south-western states of the USA, Mexico, Central America and the West Indies, there is considerable diversity, and at various times during its history groups of species, or even single species, have been split away from *Mammillaria* to become separate genera. Almost inexorably, the wheel turned full circle after a time and the segregate genera were reabsorbed. Among the generic names that may still be found on labels in nurseries are *Dolichothele*, *Krainzia*, *Bartschella* and *Solisia*. Mention should also be made of *Mamillopsis* and *Cochemiea*, for which a reasonable case has been made but which have been adopted only by the avant-garde.

For newcomers, the nursery lists offer a bewildering choice. Within the confines of this small book it is possible to suggest only a limited selection, but between them these provide an indication of what the genus has to offer.

Fig 74 Mammillaria bocasana (*pink form*).

Mammillaria bocasana is one of the underrated members of the genus: occurring in almost every collection and being easy to cultivate, it is often dismissed as of little merit, yet offers much. It is rather variable, some plants having more of the silky white radial spines than others, so it is possible to select an attractive form which can, with care, be grown into a large cluster. The small, creamy yellow flowers are produced in profusion and are usually followed by long, slender, bright-red fruits, which persist for many weeks.

There are numerous variants of *Mammillaria elongata*, differing in the colour of the spination which varies from almost white through shades of yellow and brown to chocolate. Several of these have been given varietal names, but the justification for these has disappeared as knowledge of the natural variation has been gained. The plant has a distinctive appearance, with slender, finger-like stems, and can be grown into a large clump. Yellow flowers are produced in whorls around the ends of the stems.

Mammillaria bombycina is another that will eventually grow into a very large specimen. This too has elongated stems, but they are thicker than those of *M. elongata*. The attraction lies in the contrast between the stout central spines, one of which is hooked, the numerous slender radial spines and the dense white wool which fills the space between the tubercles. The flowers of *M. bombycina* are small and purple in colour.

White-spined plants have a fascination all their own, and there are many species which combine white spines with a very neat and geometrical arrangement of the areoles which adds to their appeal. Pre-eminent among these are two plants. The first was once known as *Mammillaria elegans*, but this name has been superseded by *Mammillaria haageana*. This is usually a solitary plant, though it sometimes forms clusters in age, with a few dark central spines and many white radial spines. The flowers of *M. haageana* are purplish-pink.

The second plant, *Mammillaria geminispina*, exhibits considerable variation in the length of the central spines. These are white, tipped with

Fig 75 Mammillaria gracilis.

Fig 76 Mammillaria hahniana.

Fig 77 Mammillaria magnimamma.

brown, and as the radial spines are also white a large clump of a long-spined form is spectacular. Unfortunately, this species is reluctant to produce its small purplish flowers in cultivation.

Another white-spined plant that suffers from its extreme ease of propagation by being dismissed by 'serious' collectors, is *Mammillaria gracilis*. It is a small species, individual heads being no more than 1in (2.5cm) in diameter, which offsets prolifically. The offsets are only loosely attached, so rough handling while repotting produces many cuttings which quickly root. The result is that small plants of *M. gracilis* turn up at school fêtes and similar functions, where they may be purchased for a few pence. The plant is nevertheless worthy of attention. The radial spines are chalk-white, while the longer central spines, which are only produced on mature stems, are tipped with black. The small flowers are yellowish.

Mammillaria hahniana is notable for the white hair produced from between its tubercles. The plant is variable: some forms remain solitary while others cluster, and the length and density of the hair covering varies from short and scanty to long and luxurious. A good form with a dense covering of long hair and crowned with a halo of purplish-red flowers is a handsome sight.

While plants with dense spination and hair are obviously attractive, the species with a more open habit should not be overlooked: they are equally representative of the genus. Some of the species with large, fat tubercles and few spines have a charm of their own, and one of the most attractive is *Mammillaria magnimamma*. This is a variable species which may remain solitary or form large clumps, the spines may be straight or curved and the flowers may be yellow or magenta.

In addition to the easily acquired and cultivated species described above, there are many others equally suitable. Seed is available and, as the plants grow readily, this is an interesting and inexpensive way of increasing a collection.

Matucana

This Peruvian genus is among a group that has posed taxonomic problems, for which the suggested solution has been to place them all within *Borzicactus*. This suggestion has not yet found wide acceptance, however, and the plants are still more often seen labelled *Matucana*. For this reason the generic name is maintained here. It is also convenient to include with it the segregate genus *Submatucana*.

There are undoubtedly more published names than there are distinct species. As continuing study reveals links between existing 'species', the number of accepted names reduces. There are still, however, sufficiently distinct forms to attract the collector.

Matucana haynei is a handsome plant. Short and cylindrical, reaching 12in (30cm) in height, it is densely covered by white radial spines through which the stouter and darker central spines protrude. The zygomorphic (unsymmetrical) flowers are produced from the apex of the stem. They are red and about 2½in (6cm) in length. Some forms of *M. haynei* flower when about 2in (5cm) in diameter, but others seem to need to be much larger.

Fig 78 Matucana haynei.

The next species has been placed in both *Matucana* and *Submatucana*, but it appears more at home in the latter as *Submatucana paucicostata*. It provides a complete contrast with *M. haynei*, having a clustering habit. The individual bodies are dull green and are armed with short, curved spines. The plant flowers freely while young, producing tubular crimson flowers from the top.

Submatucana intertexta has also been placed in *Matucana* but is rarely labelled as such. It is a larger-growing plant than *S. paucicostata*, and may eventually reach 7in (18cm) in diameter. Its flowers are a curious mixture of red and yellow.

Neoporteria

The modern concept of *Neoporteria* embraces a number of generic names which will still be encountered frequently. These include among others *Pyrrhocactus*, *Horridocactus* and *Neochilenia*. The plants come from southern Peru, Chile and western Argentina, and exhibit a fascinating variety of forms. Some are squat, globular plants, others become columnar with age and some cluster. Some are heavily armed with long, stout spines, while others are almost spineless. Some produce large, pale-coloured and funnel-shaped flowers during the summer, while others bloom in the winter, producing much smaller, brightly coloured flowers. The species described below illustrate the diversity to be found.

Neoporteria (Neochilenia) napina has a tuberous rootstock, on top of which is a small, flattened globular body. As is the case with many of the species in this group, the body colour is dark – in this instance greyish. The black spines are tiny, only a millimetre or so long, but the funnel-shaped, pale-cream flowers are large.

In the same group, *Neoporteria (Neochilenia)*

Fig 79 Neoporteria napina.

paucicostata is a more heavily armed plant. Two forms are commonly seen: one has a dark-green body but that of the more attractive form is a distinct blue-green. To contrast with this, long, black, curved spines envelop the body and large, whitish flowers crown the plant.

Neoporteria subgibbosa is a typical member of the group, producing smaller but more brightly coloured flowers. Usually the plants are solitary and have dark-coloured bodies densely covered with stout spines which partly conceal the stem and often prevent the flowers from opening fully. The flowers are produced from the apex during the winter, thus providing colour when most cacti are resting.

In contrast, the spination of *Neoporteria gerocephala* is soft and curling, interlacing to form an impenetrable covering. The spines vary in colour, in some forms being white but more usually darker.

Members of the *Horridocactus* group produce flowers in unusual colours. Those of *Neoporteria (Horridocactus) tuberisulcatus* are of a distinctive brownish colour, while those of *Neoporteria curvispinus* are straw-coloured. In general appearance the plants resemble the pink-flowered *Neoporteria* species, though they have a tendency to offset more readily.

Notocactus

This South American genus includes plants of very different habit and flower form, and this has led to the creation of other genera to house them. Conservative taxonomy in recent years has returned these segregates to *Notocactus*, though plants may still be found labelled with the discarded generic names. No collection should be without a representative selection of species. The plants are made desirable by their range of body form and spination, accompanied by their reliable flowering habit. Flower colours range from shades of yellow through orange, red and pink to purple.

The group of small-flowered plants includes two similar but contrasting species that were once placed in the genus *Brasilicactus*. Both have spherical bodies reaching 4–6in (10–15cm) in diameter, densely covered with slender spines about ½in (1–2cm) long, and produce small flowers from the crown early in the year. In *Notocactus graessneri* the spination is yellow and the flower is an unusual greenish-yellow, while *Notocactus haselbergii* has white spines and orange-scarlet flowers.

The most obviously columnar species is *Notocactus leninghausii*, once placed in *Eriocactus*. This genus also included other species which become columnar in the wild though cultivated specimens remain globular. *N. leninghausii* is a beautiful plant with stems about 4in (10cm) in diameter and growing to 3ft (1m) in height. It offsets from the base to produce a clump of parallel stems clad with thin, yellow spines. Large, yellow flowers are produced from the growing point, often when the plant is only 4in (10cm) or so tall.

Another member of the *Eriocactus* group is one of the outstanding discoveries of recent years. The aptly-named *Notocactus magnificus*

Fig 80 Notocactus graessneri.

was discovered in Brazil and introduced into cultivation during the 1960s. It is an outstandingly beautiful plant with a globular, blue-green body, divided by sharply angled ribs. The yellow spines are slender and accompanied by white wool, particularly on the younger growth. Sometimes the plant remains solitary, but sometimes it forms large clumps. Large, yellow flowers are produced from the apex. This species should be kept slightly warm during the coldest part of the year to avoid marking.

Collectors are sometimes alarmed when one of these four species begins to grow unsymmetrically so that the crown of the plant is inclined at an angle. This is a perfectly natural phenomenon, however, and although some growers go to a lot of trouble to rotate the plant relative to the incident light at frequent intervals, there is no point in doing so.

Notocactus scopa is a small plant with neat spination which may be pure white, a mixture of red and white, or a mixture of yellow and brown. Not surprisingly, many of these variants have

Fig 81 Notocactus leninghausii.

Fig 82 Notocactus uebelmannianus.

received names, but as they gradually merge into one another in the habitat (and several may be isolated from a batch of seedlings) the distinction cannot be maintained. The flowers of this species are small and yellow.

Other species of *Notocactus* have globular bodies and large flowers. *Notocactus mammulosus* has a glossy green body, short spines and yellow flowers. *Notocactus horstii* has longer spines and orange flowers. *Notocactus ottonis* and its varieties often produce clumps of small bodies. Most varieties have yellow flowers, but var. *vencluisianus* has bright-orange flowers.

Notocactus uebelmannianus is another recent introduction. Its body closely resembles that of a Gymnocalycium, though its true identity is revealed when the furry Notocactus buds appear. The flowers may be yellow or, in the most popular and fortunately most common form, a rich purple.

Although Notocacti do not offer particular difficulty in cultivation, the grower should be aware of a few potential problems. Several species have a distressing habit of becoming corky at the base. This is natural, but sometimes the corkiness steadily spreads up the body until only the top part is unmarked. There seems to be no way of preventing or curing this: the only solution is to have a younger plant growing on as a replacement. It is also advisable to give Notocacti a small amount of water during the winter to prevent loss of roots due to excessive desiccation, as these plants are often difficult to re-establish.

Opuntia

This huge genus, together with its segregates, contains plants ranging from large trees to small, mat-forming species. Unfortunately, the number that are suitable for indoor cultivation is restricted. Some rapidly grow too large to be accommodated. Others are armed with vicious barbed spines, an encounter with which would discourage all but the most ardent enthusiasts. Of those small enough to be accommodated, few will flower in cultivation. However, the group is an important element of the Family and should be represented in a collection.

One approach might be to grow an example of the large, flat-padded type of *Opuntia* for a few years, replacing it at intervals with a rooted cutting. Usually there is no difficulty in rooting detached pads after allowing them to callus for a few days.

Another approach might be to grow a few of the smaller species, selected for their attractive appearance, regarding the production of flowers as an unexpected bonus. Among these, *Opuntia microdasys* can be recommended. It grows to about 18in (0.5m) in height, branching freely, but can be kept within limits by judicious pruning. The pads are light green, with prominent areoles containing clusters of barbed bristles (glochids) which may be yellow, white or brown. Although these appear innocuous, this is deceptive. Brushing against the plants leaves hundreds of glochids embedded in the skin, where they are both irritant and difficult to extract. The cultivar 'Angels' Wings' is a smaller-growing plant which

Fig 83 Opuntia paediophila.

has glochids without barbs, making it safe to handle, and it has the additional advantage that it flowers freely.

Opuntia articulata, frequently labelled *Tephrocactus articulatus*, and its several varieties are attractive plants with short-jointed stems and papery spines. The related *Opuntia paediophila* grows taller and has stiffer spines. Both have a tendency to shed branches if they are allowed to become too dry, and they should be given some water during the winter.

Oreocereus

In spite of attempts to submerge it within *Borzicactus*, the generic name *Oreocereus* persists and is maintained here for convenience. The plants are unlikely to flower in cultivation, even though they may reach the size of mature plants in the wild, so it appears that a vital ingredient is lacking from the conditions we provide. These are Andean plants, occurring in northern Chile, southern Peru, Bolivia and northern Argentina and growing at altitudes of up to 16,000ft (5,000m). There they are subjected to low temperatures, being covered by snow for part of the year. It is possible that the light intensity at high altitudes is the ingredient required to promote flowering.

Several names have been published, but it is debatable whether these are tenable: possibly they relate to variants of the single species *Oreocereus celsianus*. Other names that will be encountered include *Oreocereus trollii*, *Oreocereus fossulatus*, *Oreocereus maximus* and *Oreocereus hendriksenianus*, nowadays considered to be varieties of *O. celsianus*.

At first the body is club-shaped, becoming columnar with age, though growth is slow. The plants often branch to form groups of stout stems. The beauty of these plants lies in the covering of silky white hair, completely concealing the stem, protruding through which are stout, brightly coloured spines.

The Oreocerei are robust plants of easy cultivation, adding a height dimension to a collection and contrasting with the globular plants. The hair provides a refuge for pests such as mealy bugs and red spider mites, which can do a great deal of damage while masked from view, so it is advisable to inspect the plants carefully from time to time.

Oroya

This genus of three species is named after the Peruvian village near which the first plant was found. Subsequent exploration resulted in the discovery of other forms, some of which were given species names, but the majority of these have since been absorbed into the most frequently encountered species, *Oroya peruviana*.

This has a globular body, reaching about 6in (15cm) in diameter, initially solitary but sometimes forming clusters with age. The ribs are divided into large, rounded tubercles, each of which carries a neat cluster of short spines arising from an elongated areole. The short, funnel-shaped flowers, a lovely bright pink with a yellowish base, are produced from the upper part of the stem.

This species grows well from seed and soon makes a handsome specimen. Flowering performance is a little unpredictable: some young plants flower freely but sometimes much more mature specimens resolutely refuse to perform. It may be that light intensity is a factor, so plants should be positioned in the sunniest spot available.

Parodia

This South American genus contains many small growing and free-flowering species, and others of larger proportions and more majestic appearance that are sometimes reluctant to flower. Among the larger-growing species, *Parodia maassii* is outstanding. It is a robust plant, forming a globular to slightly elongated body up to 6in (15cm) in diameter and carrying an armament of hooked spines up to 2½in (6cm) long, which may be pale yellow, brown or nearly black. The flowers, red or orange, often appear on quite small specimens though the species has a reputation of being shy-flowering. Several of the new discoveries of recent years are considered by some authorities to be closely related to this species and are often labelled as varieties of *P. maassii*. These include *Parodia maxima*, *Parodia commutans*, *Parodia rubida* and *Parodia subterranea*.

Parodia penicillata grows to a similar size but has straight, pale-coloured spines. The ribs are divided into prominent tubercles carrying an areole at the tip from which the spines project like the bristles of a brush. The flowers are red, sometimes of a distinctive flame-red shade.

Another straight-spined species, popular with exhibitors, is *Parodia chrysacanthion*. This has a flattened globular body densely covered with long, golden spines and with white wool in the younger areoles near the apex. The small, yellow flowers, produced from the crown, are less showy than those of other species.

Among the smaller-growing species are several of very neat appearance, with spiralling ribs, straight radial spines and one or more short, hooked central spines. The yellow-flowered *Parodia mutabilis* has central spines that may be any colour from white through yellow, orange, pink and red to black. *Parodia microsperma* has yellow flowers, while those of the aptly-named var. *rubriflora* are red. *Parodia sanguiniflora* also lives up to its name, having blood-red flowers.

Patience is required to raise Parodias from seed, particularly the smaller-growing types. Although germination is normally good, growth is initially extremely slow. It is usually a year or so before the seedlings are large enough for pricking out. Once they reach the size of peas, the growth rate seems to increase. These species also have a rather weak root system and care should be taken that they do not dry out too much in the resting period. The larger-growing types such as *P. maassii* grow much more vigorously from seed and are easier at all stages of growth.

Rebutia

The genus *Rebutia*, as currently accepted, includes several genera that were erected on the basis of relatively small differences in characteristics. Among these, the names most likely to be found are *Aylostera* and *Mediolobivia*. These are mountain plants, confined to the eastern side of the Andes in north-western Argentina and Bolivia, where they grow at altitudes between 5,000 and 13,000ft (1,500–4,000m).

They are superb flowering plants, often producing their first blooms when less than ½in (1cm) or so in diameter and less than a year old. Flowers are usually produced in profusion from close to the base of the stems. The colour range embraces white, shades of yellow, orange, pink, red, lilac and purple. The majority have globular bodies, often offsetting to produce large clumps, while a few have elongated stems about the thickness of a finger.

Most Rebutias grow readily and quickly from seed, and they pose few problems in cultivation.

Some have rather soft bodies and seem to attract red spider mite, and it is advisable to keep a close watch for this pernicious pest.

The first species discovered, just before the end of the last century, was *Rebutia minuscula* and, although more striking plants have been introduced since, this is still worthy of a place in a collection for its ease of growth and free-flowering habit. The dull-green, flattened globular bodies are about 2in (5cm) in diameter, clustering freely and protected by a weak armament of soft spines. The flowers are red, but ssp. *violaciflora* has pale-violet flowers.

Rebutia senilis is a rather similar plant but with denser spination, and in its various forms it exhibits a wider range of flower colour, including red (*senilis*), orange (*iseliniana*), lilac-red (*lilacina-rosea*) and yellow (*kesselringiana*).

The tiniest species is *Rebutia albiflora*, which has bodies only about ½in (10–15mm) in diameter but offsets prolifically to produce large mats within a short time. The pink buds appear early in the year and open as white flowers.

Among the relatively recent discoveries are several that have quickly become favourites with collectors. *Rebutia muscula* (not to be confused with *R. minuscula*) is a beautiful plant, densely covered with white spines and having flowers of a bright-orange colour. If it has a fault, it is its habit of leaning to one side when about to offset so that an untidy clump is produced. *Rebutia narvaecensis* is more likely to be found labelled with the invalid name *Rebutia espinosae*. This is a worthy addition to any collection by virtue of its freely produced pale-pink flowers.

The species with the most attractive spination is undoubtedly *Rebutia heliosa*. This small-bodied plant has elongated areoles from which short, silvery spines radiate in pectinate fashion. The plant clusters freely and when enveloped in bright-orange flowers is a magnificent sight. A close second in the attractive-spination stakes must be *Rebutia krainziana*, an old favourite, with clusters of very short, white spines making an

Fig 84 Rebutia muscula.

Fig 85 Rebutia narvaecensis.

effective contrast with the dark-green body. The flowers are normally scarlet, but occasionally an attractive orange-flowered form may be seen.

The types with elongated stems, often labelled *Mediolobivia*, are usually slower-growing than the globular forms. Among the most attractive is *Rebutia pygmaea* with a dark body, short spines, and flowers of a colour somewhere between pink and salmon.

Schlumbergera

It is convenient to group with this genus both *Zygocactus*, now considered to be synonymous with *Schlumbergera*, and the related and rather similar *Rhipsalidopsis*. They are epiphytic cacti, having their origins in the Brazilian rain forest, but the plants offered for sale in garden centres, chainstores and other outlets, the popular

Fig 86 Schlumbergera *hybrid.*

'Christmas Cactus' and 'Easter Cactus', are products of the hybridists' skill.

They are available in a bewildering range of flower colours that includes reds, oranges, whites and – a recent introduction – yellow. Usually they do not carry a cultivar name, and are acquired in bud or flower as houseplants.

Their cultural requirements are quite different from those of other cacti. They need a compost containing a large proportion of humus in the form of peat or leafmould. It is important that the compost should remain moist but not waterlogged at all times, and it is advisable to use rainwater if that is available. The plants do not enjoy the hot, dry conditions of a cactus house and grow much better indoors.

Sulcorebutia

This genus was created as recently as 1951 to contain the one species recognised at that time, *Sulcorebutia steinbachii*. Since then, exploration of the mountains of south-western Bolivia has resulted in the naming of nearly fifty species. Some of these exhibit variability which suggests that further research will lead to a reduction in the number of names.

These are attractive plants, similar in general appearance to the related *Rebutia*. Intensive propagation for a demanding market means that grafted plants are often offered for sale, which may suggest to the uninitiated that they pose cultural difficulties. This is not the case: the plants grow just as well on their own roots and certainly look much more attractive.

Most of the species have elongated areoles and a pectinate spine cluster. Flowers are produced from the base and sides of the stem and closely resemble those of *Rebutia*. They are, however, more intensely coloured. Cultivation requirements are similar to those of *Rebutia*.

Sulcorebutia arenacea is one of the most

Fig 87 Sulcorebutia arenacea.

distinctive species with a dark-green body, spiralling ribs carrying short, brownish spines and bright-yellow flowers. *Sulcorebutia candiae* is another yellow-flowered species, but with somewhat longer spines.

Among the species with red or purplish flowers are many with spination which varies from specimen to specimen, and this may give the impression that the plants are of different species. For example, some forms of *Sulcorebutia crispata* have short spines closely following the body contours, while others have longer and more protruding spines. Its flowers are magenta. *S. steinbachii* is another variable species with several varieties distinguished by their spination. *S. steinbachii* var. *gracilior* has short, slender spines arranged in pectinate fashion, while var. *horrida* has long, stout spines and could easily be mistaken for a *Neoporteria* when not in flower. Perhaps the most appropriately named variety is var. *polymorpha*, meaning 'many forms'.

The flowers of *Sulcorebutia canigueralii* are among the most striking, being yellow at the base and red at the outer part. The body is also very attractive, as the tiny spines wrap themselves closely around the tubercles. The outstanding member of the genus, however, is *Sulcorebutia rauschii*. There are several forms of this species, the best having a purplish body with flattened tubercles carrying long areoles with short, black spines and producing flowers of a deep-purple colour.

Thelocactus

No collection should be without a few representatives of this genus. The plants are widely available as seedlings, or may be grown easily and quickly from seed to flowering size. There is a reasonable range of body form and spination, and the large, showy flowers are freely produced on small plants. Given normal compost, a position in full sun and adequate water when in growth, they can be expected to produce their showy flowers every year. The genus occurs in

Fig 88 Sulcorebutia rauschii.

Fig 89 Thelocactus conothelos.

the wild in Mexico and across the border in Texas.

The best-known species is *Thelocactus bicolor*, a ribbed plant growing to about 4in (10cm) in diameter, occasionally offsetting to form a small clump. The spines are stout and attractively coloured red and yellow, fading to greyish-white. The flowers are striking, about 2½in (6cm) across, bright pink with a reddish throat and with a beautiful satiny sheen.

Thelocactus hexaedrophorus is a plant of very different appearance. The body is globular or slightly flattened, with large, humped tubercles, while the areoles carry only a few stout spines, straight or curving back towards the body. The flowers, similar in size to *T. bicolor*, are white.

The body of the larger-growing *Thelocactus lophothele* is divided into more slender tubercles carrying a few straight, dark-coloured spines. Its flowers are pale yellow, fading to a pinkish colour. The varieties of *Thelocactus conothelos* offer a contrast in flower colour. Those of var. *conothelos* and var. *mcdowellii* are purple, while var. *aurantiacus* has yellow flowers.

Trichocereus

Trichocereus schickendantzii grows to less than 18in (0.5m) but branches prolifically to form a clump of upright green stems with short, white spines. It is possible to flower this species while still quite small: a stem 4in (10cm) high carrying a white flower over 8in (20cm) long is a spectacular sight.

Trichocereus pasacana is a larger-growing species reaching over 30ft (10m) in the wild but growing slowly in cultivation, where it produces a massive stem with stout, golden spines. The flowers are white but are unlikely to be produced on cultivated plants. Like the preceding species, it comes from the eastern side of the Andes in South America.

A plant from the western side of the Andes is the Chilean *Trichocereus fulvilanus*, one of the most rewarding in the genus. Young plants are extremely attractive with green stems, large areoles with orange-brown felt and stout spines which are initially dark brown with yellow bases but fade to grey with age. The plant offsets from the base to form a cluster of upright stems which may reach 3ft (1m) or so. Short-tubed, white flowers, darker on the outside of the petals, about 3in (8cm) in diameter are produced from near the top of the stems. The plant flowers reliably once it reaches about 18in (0.5m) in height.

It is important to provide these plants and other columnar types with adequate root room. Although it is often possible to accommodate them in small pots, they will not grow satisfactorily under such conditions.

Turbinicarpus

This is another Mexican genus that has enjoyed (or suffered from) the attentions of taxonomists. The 'traditional' species were segregated from *Strombocactus* as a coherent group, which was then enlarged by the inclusion of several other dwarf cacti. Recently there has been a move to return them to *Strombocactus*, but since the species described here are of the 'traditional' group and likely to be acquired labelled *Turbinicarpus*, it is convenient to identify them as such.

They form a small group of dwarf plants, although some specimens offset to produce modest clumps. As they begin to flower early in the year and produce a succession of blooms through to the autumn, they have much to commend them, particularly where space is limited.

Turbinicarpus schmiedickeanus var. *schwarzii*, often labelled *Turbinicarpus schwarzii*, begins to flower when about two years old. It has a small, flattened globular body, grey-green in colour, with broad, flat tubercles carrying one or two soft spines. White flowers, about 1½in (4cm) in diameter, are produced from the apex. *Turbinicarpus macrochele* is rather similar, but with longer, curved spines, and produces a small amount of white wool in the crown of the plant.

Turbinicarpus pseudomacrochele, with slender,

Fig 90 Turbinicarpus pseudomacrochele.

curved, yellowish spines, is more vigorous and often forms small clusters. Its flowers may be white, pink, or white with a pink midstripe and at about 1½in (4cm) in diameter are the most attractive in the group.

These plants have an unjustified reputation for difficulty. Given a gritty compost and a position in full sun, preferably on a shelf beneath the glass, they thrive. Care should be taken not to overwater them, particularly in the early part of the year when the plants may take up so much water that they split.

Weingartia

Although quite distinct in general appearance and flowering characteristics, this genus is considered to be closely related to *Sulcorebutia*, and some taxonomists would go so far as to merge the two genera. It is convenient to treat it separately here as the species likely to be encountered are easily recognised.

Weingartia neocumingii is the species most likely to be seen, but there are several others of more attractive appearance that are worth seeking out. *Weingartia pilcomayensis* has a globular body, reaching 5in (12cm) or so in diameter, with large, rounded tubercles. The areoles are large and carry, in addition to stout, brown-tipped spines, large tufts of white wool. The flowers of *W. pilcomayensis* are yellow, as they are in most of the other species.

Weingartias respond to cultivation similar to that for Sulcorebutias. A distinction of this genus, almost unique among the cacti, is its habit of producing two or more flowers to an areole.

CHAPTER 6

Other Succulents

AGAVACEAE

The Family Agavaceae contains a number of large-growing plants and relatively few of sufficiently modest proportions to be accommodated in a small greenhouse. Among the latter, two genera are included here: *Agave* and *Sansevieria*.

Agave

This genus has a distribution extending from the southern USA, through Central America and the West Indies into northern South America. The plants form rosettes, usually of tough, fibrous leaves, and may be solitary or offsetting from the base. They are monocarpic, the rosette dying after flowering, but the build-up to the production of the spectacular inflorescence can take many years. It was this property that gained the early introductions to Europe the appellation 'Century Plant', the mistaken belief being that the plant flowered once in a century.

Most members of the genus eventually become too large for convenient cultivation, though they can be kept within bounds for a few years by starvation treatment. In this category are the cultivars of *Agave americana*, some with yellow or white central stripes and others with yellow or white margins to their blue-green leaves.

More suitable are the small-growing species. *Agave victoriae-reginae* from Coahuila, Mexico, grows slowly until after many years the rosette may reach 18in (0.5m) in diameter. The leaves vary from pale to dark green, are attractively marked with white and have a sharp tip. The rosettes may be solitary or offsetting, the latter form often being labelled *Agave fernandi-regis*.

The leaves of several species carry white filaments on their edges which enhance their appearance. The Mexican *Agave filifera* forms a rosette about 18in (0.5m) across of slender leaves edged with untidy filaments and carrying a sharp terminal spike. *Agave toumeyana* is similar in size but offsets freely. The most attractive species is *Agave parviflora*, which is smaller and altogether neater in appearance.

They are easy plants to cultivate, being tolerant of any kind of compost and apparently happy whether in shade or sun. Miniature forms of the species mentioned here are sometimes offered for sale and these are well worth acquiring as they display all the symmetry and beauty of the larger forms in a fraction of the space.

Sansevieria

The species of this genus most frequently encountered are those sold as houseplants, in particular the unkindly named 'Mother-in-law's Tongue', *Sansevieria trifasciata*.

S. trifasciata is available in a number of forms. Var. *laurentii* has long, strap-like leaves edged with yellow and growing to over 3ft (1m) in length. The plant spreads by means of underground rhizomes and in a pot soon produces a dense clump of leaves. The cultivars 'Hahnii', 'Golden Hahnii' and 'Silver Hahnii' are rosette-forming plants with green leaves carrying gold or silver markings.

The Sansevierias are excellent houseplants, usually growing better on a windowsill than in a greenhouse. They are easily propagated, either

Fig 91 Agave parviflora.

by cutting through the rhizomes to isolate shoots or from leaf cuttings. With the latter method the plantlets of the variegated forms do not inherit the variegation.

ASCLEPIADACEAE

The milkweed Family contains a large number of genera, including *Ceropegia* and a group known collectively as the Stapeliads. This latter group includes plants which have some of the most fascinating flowers of all succulents, but which are also among the most difficult to cultivate.

They provide a challenge even to experienced growers. They are stem succulents, usually spreading by branching and rooting as they go. They are intolerant of a wet compost, so should be planted in a very porous gritty mixture, but they should not be allowed to dry out completely otherwise the fleshy roots will wither. The Stapeliads are sometimes affected by a fungus which manifests itself as black patches on the stems, spreading rapidly through the vascular tissue. Regular use of a systemic fungicide will discourage attack, but if black patches are seen it is safest to destroy the plant before the fungus spreads to others. Root mealy bugs can also be a problem, thriving in the open compost and congregating at the base of the stems. A soil insecticide will discourage the pests, but if a plant appears to be making no progress it is worth inspecting the roots.

The range of plants available from commercial sources varies from time to time, making it difficult to recommend particular species. The genera most likely to be offered are *Caralluma*, *Duvalia*, *Huernia*, *Piaranthus* and *Stapelia*.

Caralluma

This genus is widespread in the Old World, extending from the Canary Islands across much of southern and eastern Africa and Arabia to India. Among the most attractive species are those with strongly toothed stems, carrying

Fig 92 Caralluma hesperidum.

Fig 93 Caralluma europaea.

purplish or brownish markings on a grey-green background. *Caralluma hesperidum* from Morocco is of this type, and has five-lobed, blackish-purple flowers carried in clusters along the stems. *Caralluma dummeri* from Kenya and Tanzania has similar but more slender stems and larger flowers of a bright yellow-green colour.

The variable *Caralluma europaea* occurs as far north as southern Spain but also along the North African coast. This species has squarish stems, often branching from below ground. The flowers are small, about ½in (15mm) in diameter, with irregular transverse markings in a combination of brown, purple or reddish with cream, yellow or green.

Duvalia

The species of *Duvalia* likely to be encountered are those from Cape Province, South Africa. Although a number of names are recognised, the plants are similar in general appearance. The stems are short and oval, offsetting one from another to form long chains which remain prostrate and eventually producing large mats. The flowers are small, purplish-brown and with the lobes often folded back so that the flowers resemble a wheel hub with five radiating spokes. The names most commonly seen include *Duvalia compacta*, *Duvalia elegans* and *Duvalia reclinata*.

Huernia

The genus has a wider distribution than *Duvalia*, extending from Nigeria through southern and eastern Africa and also occurring in the Arabian subcontinent. With a few exceptions, the plants form clumps of stems about 1in (2.5cm) tall. The stems may be round or square in cross-section, five-angled with soft teeth or tuberculate and, depending on the growing conditions provided, green, purplish-red or attractively marbled with purple on a greyish ground. The flowers, ranging up to about 2in (5cm) in diameter, vary considerably in shape and colour.

One of the most attractive is *Huernia hystrix*,

Fig 94 Huernia primulina.

Fig 95 Huernia zebrina.

with five-angled stems carrying teeth that are quite hard to the touch. The flowers have the faces of the lobes covered with slender excrescences (papillae) and are yellow with irregular reddish lines. Another species with similar stems is *Huernia penzigii*, often labelled *Huernia macrocarpa* var. *penzigii*, but this has bell-shaped flowers of a uniform purple-red colour. *Huernia primulina* is a pretty species with blue-green stems up to about 3in (8cm) tall. The flowers are produced from the basal part of the stems and are a delightful primrose-yellow.

Several Huernias have flowers with a raised annulus around the centre which has earned them the collective title 'Lifebuoy Huernias'. One of the most beautiful is the variable *Huernia zebrina*, which has large flowers with lobes which may be rounded or tapering sharply to the tip and a prominent annulus. The flowers carry irregular markings which may take the form of spots or coalesce into transverse stripes of purple-red or brown on a cream or yellow ground.

There are many other members of this genus of nearly a hundred kinds that may be offered for sale, and none will disappoint.

Piaranthus

Vegetatively, this South African genus is similar to *Duvalia*, but the star-shaped flowers are more colourful. It too has more species names than can really be justified. The flower-buds usually appear in late summer and then need a period of bright sunny weather to develop.

Piaranthus parvulus has pale yellow flowers about ½in (1cm) in diameter, the smallest in the genus. Those of *Piaranthus pillansii* are three times larger and are greenish-yellow, while those of *Piaranthus globosus* are intermediate between

Fig 96 Piaranthus globosus.

the other two, with reddish markings on a yellow ground.

The flowers of the Stapeliads have an undeserved reputation for having a foul smell, giving rise to the popular name 'Carrion Flowers', which attracts insect pollinators. While some flowers are indeed unpleasantly scented (the perfumes have been likened to rotting meat, fresh manure and open drains), those of the majority are inoffensive. The aptly-named *Piaranthus foetidus* is one of the exceptions: its dark, often almost black, flowers have a powerful scent.

Stapelia

This is another large genus, occurring from South Africa into East Africa, and it exhibits an interesting range of flower sizes, shapes and colours. *Stapelia gigantea* is one of the contenders for the distinction of having the largest flower in the plant kingdom. Its yellow flowers, marked with narrow red lines, are over 12in (30cm) in diameter.

The most widely grown species is *Stapelia variegata*, often labelled *Orbea variegata*, from Cape Province. This is an extremely variable plant with numerous forms. Typically the flower has broad, triangular lobes and a prominent annulus, and is marked with purplish-brown blotches on a yellow ground, but among the varieties can be found flowers that are almost pure yellow and others that show virtually no yellow ground. Although often discounted as common and easy, *S. variegata* is one of the most attractive members of the genus.

Another commonly encountered species is *Stapelia hirsuta*, which has square cross-section stems and an upright habit. Its flowers are about 4in (10cm) across, with tapering lobes of deep purple-brown covered with similarly coloured hairs. The perfume exuded frequently attracts

Fig 97 Stapelia variegata.

blowflies to lay their eggs on the open flower, which hatch into maggots doomed to die a lingering death.

Ceropegia

This genus of the Asclepiadaceae is related to, but is not part of, the Stapeliad group. It is a large genus with a distribution from the Canary Islands through tropical and southern Africa, Arabia, India, southern China and Indonesia to Australia. Among the various growth forms are plants with stick-like upright stems, others with thin trailing stems arising from subterranean tubers, and others that are vigorous climbers. The flowers are five-lobed, like those of the Stapeliads, but in most the tips of the lobes are joined to produce curious lantern-like structures.

The species readily available pose no difficulty in cultivation. Some are well-suited to cultivation in a basket or pot suspended from above, which will allow the pendent stems to hang down and display the flowers. The most attractive of these is *Ceropegia woodii*, a tuberous-rooted plant with slender stems bearing heart-shaped leaves, silver-grey on the upper surface and red below. Its small flowers are like narrow lanterns.

Among the larger-flowered types, *Ceropegia stapeliiformis* has stems which at the base are thick and heavily textured but which become smooth and slender as they clamber over whatever is provided for their support. The slender growth produces the flowers, which are tubular with spreading lobes and whitish with dark markings. *Ceropegia sandersonii* is another climbing species, but with uniform stems and large, green and white flowers which have the lobes joined to form a structure similar to an opened parachute.

Support for the climbing types is essential, otherwise they will wrap themselves around any other plants in their vicinity. This can be provided in the form of a ladder support of thin canes or plastic material, or the plants may be positioned at the rear of the bench and allowed to climb up suspended netting.

CRASSULACEAE

This large family of leaf succulents has a distribution spanning both hemispheres, and a range of habitats from the mountains of Europe to the deserts of southern Africa. Of approximately three dozen genera, about a third are represented in succulent plant collections.

They offer much to the collector. None grow so large as to become an embarrassment. Most are accommodating with regard to compost, temperature and watering requirements. Many have very colourful leaves and, though the flowers of some are small and insignificant, others have colourful flowers of a reasonable size. Propagation is simplicity itself. The branching types yield cuttings or ready-rooted offsets and most can be propagated from leaf cuttings.

Adromischus

Adromischus occurs in South Africa and Namibia. The plants are small and compact and many have attractively mottled leaves. Flowers are produced on stems extending well above the leaves, and although not striking they have a certain charm. To encourage the development of colour in the leaves, the plants should be positioned in a good light. They need adequate water when growing, but care should be taken that the compost does not remain wet for long periods, otherwise the fleshy roots may rot.

Adromischus maculatus has broad leaves heavily mottled with purplish-brown on a grey-green ground. This species develops a thickened stem with age. *Adromischus cooperi* is another attractively marked species, and the form often labelled *Adromischus festivus* is outstandingly pretty, with oval leaves, grey with dark purple-brown markings. In both forms the leaf tip is wavy. This characteristic is even more marked in *Adromischus cristatus*, which has dull green leaves, strongly waved at the tips, carried on short stems densely covered with reddish-brown, hairlike aerial roots. Another outstandingly pretty plant, *Adromischus leucophyllus* has its leaves and flower-buds covered with a white bloom.

Aeonium

Most of the members of this genus found in collections hail from the Canary Isles, though the genus has a wider distribution in North Africa and on other islands off the north-west of the continent. They are rosette-forming, but some develop tall, branching stems and eventually become shrubs 3ft (1m) or so in height. When they become too tall the terminal rosettes with a short length of stem can be removed and rooted.

The plants should be grown fairly hard in good light. In shady conditions the stems become softer, the leaves elongate so that the compact shape is lost and the colouring deteriorates.

Aeonium haworthii is a shrubby plant growing to about 18in (0.5m), with thin, woody stems tipped with rosettes of bluish-green leaves, often edged with red. *Aeonium arboreum* is a taller and less branched plant with rosettes at the tips of the stems. There are several cultivars that are more attractive than the species: 'Atropurpureum' has purplish rosettes which lose their colour in the winter, 'Schwarzkopf' is a similar plant but retains its colour all year round, while 'Luteovariegatum' and 'Albovariegatum' are variegated, with yellow- and white-edged leaves respectively.

Cotyledon

At one time *Cotyledon* contained the plants now placed in *Adromischus* and *Echeveria*, but separation of these genera left a rather disparate group which recently was further rationalised by the creation of the genus *Tylecodon*. Plants will still be found bearing the older name but, as their cultural requirements are different, the two groups will be treated separately.

Cotyledon contains plants with persistent leaves and bell-shaped flowers that hang downwards. The most attractive species is *Cotyledon orbiculata* from South Africa and Namibia. This is very variable, with forms that grow to only a few centimetres tall and others that reach over 3ft (1m). The size and shape of the leaves vary from large and broad to small and narrow. Sometimes the leaves are densely covered with a white bloom, sometimes they are not. The flowers are orange-red and are carried above the leaves. *Cotyledon ladismithensis* is another shrubby plant but is of very different appearance. The stems are slender and woody, growing to about 12in (30cm) tall. The leaves are fleshy, green and covered with fine hairs, while the flowers are yellowish.

Fig 98 Cotyledon ladismithensis.

Tylecodon contains the deciduous species with flowers pointing upwards. They grow during our winter, then rest during our summer, shedding their leaves and requiring no water. As an example of the genus, *Tylecodon reticulatus* (*Cotyledon reticulata*) is recommended. This grows to about 12in (30cm), producing a stout, gnarled trunk and short branches. The yellowish-green flowers are carried on slender, woody stems which persist after the flowers wither.

Fig 99 Crassula deceptor.

Crassula

This is a large and diverse genus, containing many plants of little horticultural merit but others of instant appeal to connoisseurs. The flowers are tiny and usually pale-coloured, but sometimes are massed in a large head: in *Crassula falcata* they are bright red, making this a popular florists' plant. A few species are small trees, reaching over 10ft (3m), and even when grown in pots they aspire to this by forming a stout trunk and branches. One of the best of this type is *Crassula ovata* (frequently labelled *Crassula argentea* or *Crassula portulacea*), with green leaves sometimes edged with red. The cultivar 'Hummel's Sunset' is more colourful, having variegated red and yellow leaves.

The dwarf, highly succulent species appeal most to collectors, and there are many among which to choose. *Crassula deceptor* and *Crassula cornuta* are names attached somewhat hap-

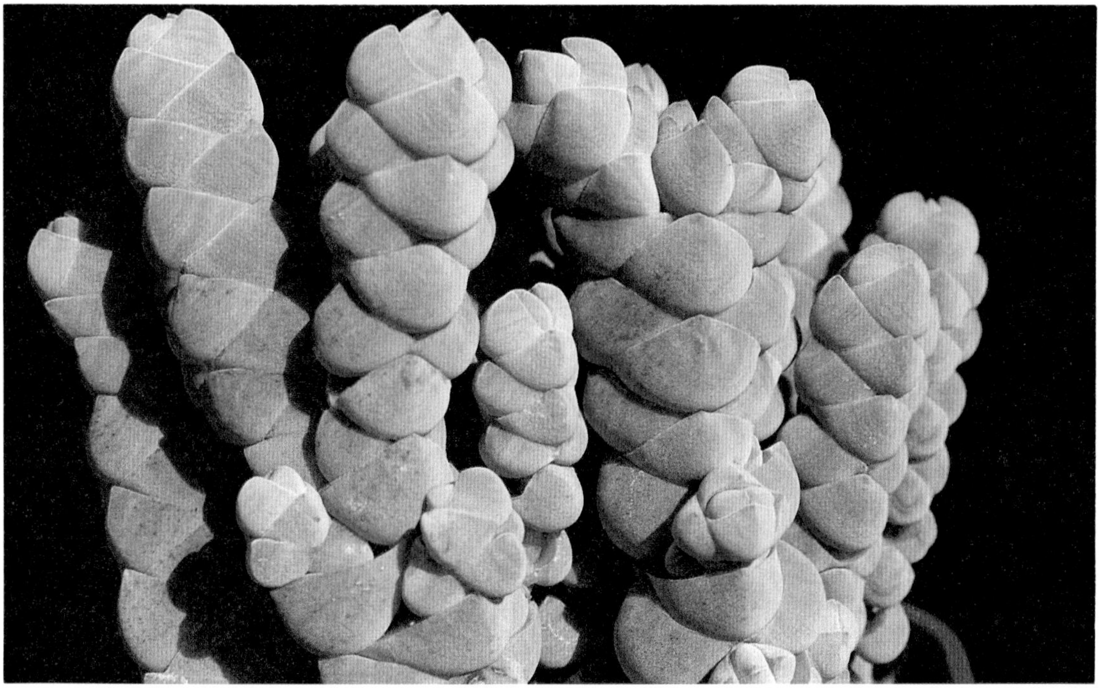

Fig 100 Crassula plegmatoides.

Fig 101 Crassula barbata.

hazardly to a group of broadly similar plants now considered to be forms of a single variable species. They form short columns of closely packed, greyish-white fleshy leaves which often have a red edge or fine red dots on the surface. Another attractive plant of similar but more robust habit and having grey-green leaves is correctly named *Crassula plegmatoides* but is more frequently labelled *Crassula arta*. *Crassula columella* is smaller, with green leaves often becoming edged with red during the resting phase.

In contrast, *Crassula barbata* has paper-thin leaves edged with long hairs, forming an almost stemless rosette. When grown in good light and watered sparingly, this plant responds by curling its leaves inwards until it has the appearance of a furry, silver ball. It usually retains this form for a relatively short period before the rosette unfolds and its centre elongates into an inflorescence of white flowers. The rosette then dies, but offsets are usually produced and can be detached for propagation.

The dwarf Crassulas should be grown in a good light if they are to retain their squat habit and develop their proper coloration. Many of them grow and flower in late winter and early spring, and appreciate a rest afterwards. If they seem not to be taking up water, the compost may be allowed to dry out, but care should be taken that the leaves do not shrivel too much. With age, many become untidy at the base as the lower leaves wither, and sometimes aerial roots are produced part way along the stems. It is advisable then to take cuttings and grow on a vigorous young plant to replace the original.

Dudleya

This genus occurs in Mexico and the south-western part of the USA. Of about sixty species, only a handful are cultivated. The most popular is *Dudleya farinosa*, a branching plant in which each stem terminates in a rosette of slender leaves densely covered with a white, waxy coating (farina). *Dudleya brittonii* grows larger, eventually forming a solitary rosette 18in (0.5m) in diameter, and also has farinaceous leaves. This farina is easily and permanently marked, so care must be exercised when handling the plants.

The older leaves of Dudleyas wither but remain attached to the stem. Whether or not they should be removed is disputed, but they provide a hiding place for pests and the author's preference is to remove them.

Echeveria

This large genus is centred on Mexico but extends into the southern part of the USA and into Central and South America. The plants are rosette-forming: some are stemless but others may produce a stout stem 3ft (1m) in height and some are semi-shrubby. In addition to about a hundred species, there are many hybrids of attractive appearance and vigour. The leaves are very colourful, ranging from white to almost black through pastel shades of green, blue and pink and darker purplish colours. The leaves are often overlaid with a waxy bloom and some are covered with fine hairs. The flower-colour range embraces yellow, orange and red.

The plants must be given space to develop. If they are packed closely together, the leaves will become marked. The tall-growing types can be kept within bounds by beheading and rooting the terminal rosette. Most also grow easily from leaf cuttings. The small leaves (bracts) produced on the flower stems are a fruitful source of new plants.

Echeveria setosa is stemless, with a densely leaved rosette reaching 4in (10cm) in diameter. The green leaves are covered with short hairs and a mature plant has the appearance of a silvery ball. Showy red and yellow flowers are carried above the rosette. *Echeveria shaviana* is another stemless or short-stemmed species, offsetting from the base. Its leaves are smooth, grey with pink margins, incurving and wavy-edged. *Echeveria pulidonis* is a pretty species with blue-

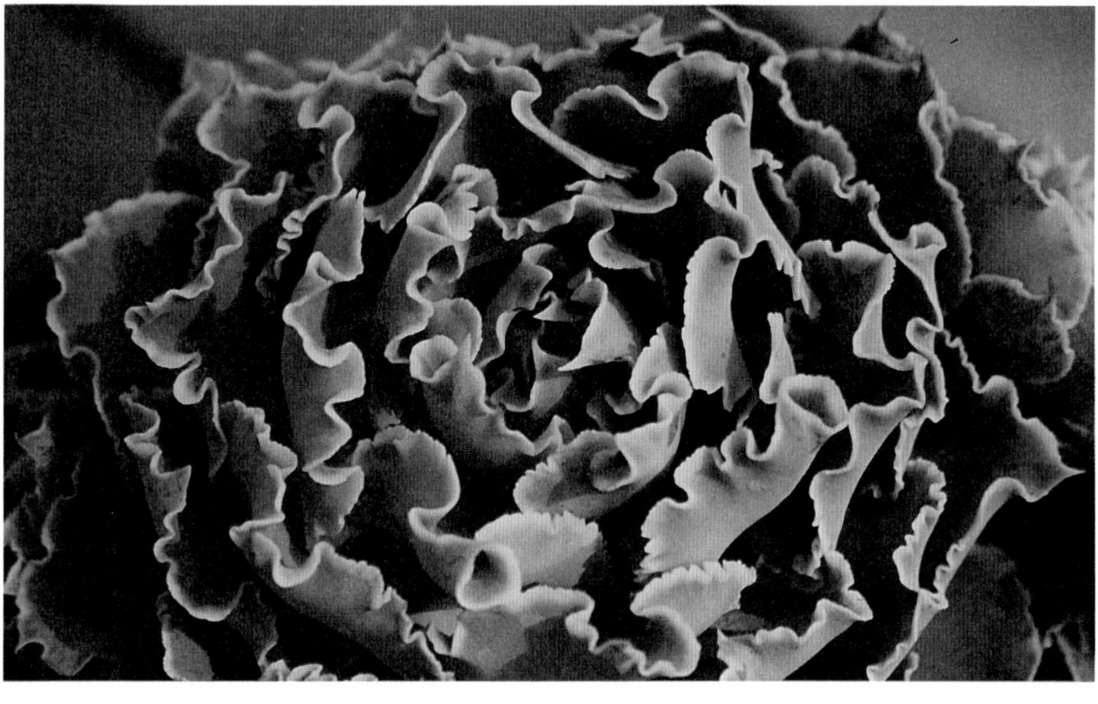

Fig 102 Echeveria shaviana.

Fig 103 Echeveria pulvinata *'Ruby'*

green leaves edged with red, which is further enhanced by its bright-yellow flowers carried on short stems. In complete contrast, *Echeveria affinis* has leaves that are almost black while its flowers are bright red.

Among the semi-shrubby types, *Echeveria leucotricha* grows to about 6in (15cm) and has leaves densely covered with silver hairs which become brown at the leaf tips. Its flowers are red. *Echeveria pulvinata* cv. 'Ruby' has a similar habit, but its stems are covered with brown felt and the leaves are green, becoming suffused with purple-red. The flowers are yellow inside, red outside, making an effective contrast with the stems and leaves.

Kalanchoe

Kalanchoe spans the tropical regions of both Old and New Worlds. The plants are often colourful and free-flowering with brightly coloured blooms, and pose no problems in cultivation. *Kalanchoe blossfeldiana* and its cultivars are popular houseplants, flowering through the winter months. *Kalanchoe diagremontiana* and *Kalanchoe tubiflora* (once placed in a separate genus, *Bryophyllum*) have a fascinating method of reproduction. They produce tiny plantlets on the edges of their leaves which eventually drop off, root and grow into new plants. They can sometimes become a nuisance in a collection, but never fail to fascinate children.

Kalanchoe pumila is a superb plant for a hanging basket, where it produces a mass of leaves covered with white farina and bright-pink flowers. *Kalanchoe tomentosa* grows upright to 18in (0.5m) or so, branching from the base. Stems and leaves are densely covered with white felt, becoming brown at the tips of the leaves.

Tacitus

This beautiful plant was one of the outstanding discoveries of the 1970s. Found in a canyon in Mexico, it was at first thought to be an *Echeveria*, then a *Graptopetalum*, and was eventually assigned to a new genus as *Tacitus bellus*. Extensively propagated, it is now freely available under one or other of these names.

Superficially similar in appearance to a small-

Fig 104 Kalanchoe pumila.

Fig 105 Tacitus bellus.

growing *Echeveria*, the rosette comprises closely packed leaves that are deep green to brownish in colour. The outstanding beauty of this plant lies in its flowers. These are carried on short stems and are brilliant red with prominent golden anthers. They also have the merit of being long-lasting.

T. bellus appreciates similar growing conditions to *Echeveria*: a reasonably rich compost and adequate water when growing and flowering. It is susceptible to fungal attack if overhead watering results in drops remaining trapped between the leaves, but otherwise it is not difficult.

EUPHORBIACEAE

The Family Euphorbiaceae is huge and cosmopolitan, with around five thousand species in its three hundred genera, but of these only a few include succulent plants and only one, *Euphorbia*, is relevant to this work.

Euphorbia

This genus has around two thousand species, of which nearly five hundred are succulent. Predominantly plants of the Old World, although a few species occur in the New World, they exhibit a diversity of form which uncannily parallels that of the cacti.

Just as many cacti have evolved a spherical shape in order to reduce water loss, so too have some species of *Euphorbia*. This reaches its ultimate expression in *Euphorbia obesa*, a globular plant from Cape Province, South Africa, which rarely exceeds 5in (12cm) in diameter. The body has broad ribs, carrying faint longitudinal and transverse lines. Flowers are produced from the apex and, although these (as in most species) are insignificant, they are worthy of inspection. *E. obesa* is dioecious, that is individual plants are either male (and produce only stamens) or female (and produce only stigmas). To set seed it

Fig 106 Euphorbia obesa.

Fig 107 Euphorbia meloformis.

is necessary to have two specimens of different sex.

Euphorbia meloformis is another globular plant from the same area, but with more pronounced ribs than *E. obesa*. It often offsets, unlike *E. obesa* which is almost invariably solitary. This species too is dioecious, but its flowers are carried on branching peduncles (flower stems) which persist after the flowers have dropped.

Looking even more like a cactus, *Euphorbia horrida* is a clustering plant which may reach 3ft (1m) in height but is usually much smaller. It has prominent, sharp-edged ribs with persistent peduncles, and strongly resembles a spiny cactus.

Contrast in form is provided by *Euphorbia pseudocactus*, a columnar and sparsely branched species. The stems exhibit a curious mode of growth. They may have three, four or five angles with a horny edge carrying pairs of spines, and grow unevenly so that they appear segmented with stout regions alternating with constricted regions. The stems are very attractive, with U-shaped, feathery markings in pale green superimposed on a darker ground.

Euphorbia mammillaris is another branching

Fig 108 Euphorbia mammillaris (*variegated form*).

plant but of smaller size. The stems are slender, with ribs divided into tubercles. An interesting variegated form is available, with stems that are partly white, sometimes becoming pinkish, and partly green.

Mention should also be made of *Euphorbia milii* from Madagascar, a shrubby type widely grown as a houseplant. Like its relative the poinsettia, this species has tiny flowers surrounded by colourful bracts. There are numerous varieties with red, pink or yellow bracts. The commonest form, with bright-red bracts, is often labelled *Euphorbia splendens*.

A large genus such as *Euphorbia* contains some species which require a little more care in cultivation than others, but those mentioned here pose no difficulties. A word of caution is necessary though. Euphorbias contain a milky sap or latex which is corrosive. When handling the plants or taking cuttings, avoid getting the latex on to the hands, from where it may be transferred to more sensitive areas of the body and cause intense pain. Merely brushing the region of the eyes with a contaminated hand can cause temporary blindness.

Fig 109 Aloe variegata.

LILIACEAE

The lily Family, which contains many familiar garden bulbs, is one of the largest in the plant kingdom with about 250 genera and nearly four thousand species. For the succulent-plant collector, the three most important genera are *Aloe*, *Gasteria* and *Haworthia*. The latter two are confined to South Africa and Namibia, but *Aloe* is more widespread throughout Africa, Arabia, Madagascar and the Atlantic islands. In addition, because of their ornamental and medicinal qualities, Aloes have been naturalised in other parts of the world.

Fig 110 Aloe aristata.

Aloe

Aloes range from rosettes no more than 1in (2.5cm) in diameter to trees 65ft (20m) high.

Where space is restricted, it will not be possible to accommodate mature plants of the larger-growing species. However, juvenile plants are often very attractive and worth cultivating for a few years before being discarded. *Aloe striata* is of this type, eventually producing a rosette 3ft (1m) across. Seedlings form a rosette of pale-green leaves with narrow longitudinal lines, the smooth margins being pink.

Aloe ferox grows to a height of about 16ft (5m) in the wild, as a single stem densely encased in withered leaves and topped by the rosette. The species name means 'fierce' and aptly describes the leaves, which are usually spiny on both surfaces, especially in young plants.

Among the smaller species from South Africa, two are both common and well suited to indoor cultivation. *Aloe variegata*, the 'Partridge Breast Aloe', has long been a popular houseplant. The rosette contains three ranks of leaves, these being green with irregular bands of white spots and edged with tiny white teeth. The tubular flowers are pinkish and are carried on stems about 12in (30cm) long. When watering, care should be taken to avoid water settling in the centre of the rosette, as this may induce rotting.

The second dwarf species is *Aloe aristata*. This species is stemless, with a compact rosette of thin leaves that have tubercles on the face and terminate in a slender, soft awn. It usually offsets very freely, but there are more attractive forms which produce only a few offsets. The inflorescence is often branched and the flowers are orange-red.

Cultivation is not difficult, provided attention is paid to the watering regime. Too dry a compost may cause root loss due to shrivelling, while a compost that is too wet may cause roots or stem base to rot. The plants are easily propagated from seed or by separation of offsets from the parent.

Gasteria

Most Gasterias are distichous, that is the leaves are arranged in two ranks in a fan-like shape, though some eventually form conventional rosettes. The flowers, carried on a long stem, are tubular like those of *Aloe* but are swollen at the base and curved. It is this feature that gives the genus its name, from the Greek word meaning 'belly'.

The smallest species, *Gasteria liliputana*, is also one of the prettiest. It forms rosettes about 3in (8cm) across and offsets freely. The leaves are dark green, spotted with white, and the bright-pink flowers are carried on stems no more than 6in (15cm) long.

Gasteria armstrongii retains its distichous habit for many years. Its leaves are short, broad and fat, giving the plant a chunky appearance.

Another rosette-forming species, *Gasteria batesiana*, has triangular leaves with a warty texture. Grown in shady conditions the leaves remain dark green, but exposure to bright sunlight causes them to become brownish with white tubercles.

Gasterias require similar growing conditions to their relatives. They may be propagated from seed or fragments of leaf which, inserted into sandy compost, will produce clusters of plantlets within a few weeks.

Haworthia

This genus contains about seventy species, sufficiently varied to make an aesthetically satisfying collection. The majority are stemless rosettes, though a few have stems 1in (2.5cm) or so in length. The rosettes of the largest species do not exceed 6in (15cm), and most are considerably smaller, though the clustering types may eventually become large clumps. Haworthias are rarely acquired as flowering plants. Although they flower freely enough, the flowers are small, whitish and usually carried on long stems. As such they do little to enhance the appeal of the plants, which usually attract attention by virtue of their neat appearance and attractively marked leaves.

Haworthia attenuata is a clustering species with slender, hard green leaves conspicuously

Fig 111 Haworthia reinwardtii v. kaffirdriftensis.

covered with white tubercles. There are several forms, the most attractive being *H. attenuata* f. *caespitosa*, in which the tubercles coalesce into transverse bands.

Haworthia reinwardtii is another variable species. Plants collected from different localities have been given varietal names and will still be found bearing them, though it is now accepted that most of these names are superfluous. *H. reinwardtii* is a long-stemmed species with fairly small and closely packed leaves. The leaves carry tubercles like those of *H. attenuata*.

Somewhat similar, *Haworthia glauca* has harder leaves which terminate in a sharp point. They vary through the seasons, being green or blue-green when the plant is growing and assuming a purplish cast during the resting period. There are several varieties which will often be found labelled *Haworthia armstrongii*, *Haworthia herrei*, *Haworthia eilyae*, *Haworthia jonesiae* or *Haworthia jacobseniana*.

Another hard-leaved species of very different appearance is *Haworthia limifolia*. This has a

Fig 112 Haworthia retusa.

broad, flat rosette of triangular leaves which twist so that the plant looks as though it has been screwed into the ground. Both surfaces of the leaves carry narrow transverse ridges.

In contrast, some Haworthias have soft, fleshy leaves. The freely offsetting *Haworthia batesiana* is of this type, with small rosettes of bright-green leaves. Its flowers are carried on short stems, and a flowering clump is an attractive sight.

A few species have very fat leaves with 'windows' in the upper surface, enabling the plant to photosynthesise while withdrawn into the soil in the habitat. These, the so-called 'retuse' types, have great appeal. Apart from *Haworthia retusa*, which gives its name to the group, it is possible to find other attractive species such as *Haworthia emelyae*, *Haworthia pygmaea* and *Haworthia mirabilis*, though these tend to be rather expensive to purchase.

Coming from South Africa, the genus would be growing in the habitat during our winter. While most species will reverse their growing season to coincide with our summer, a few prefer to grow during our winter and rest during our summer. Observation of the plants will identify the 'awkward' ones, which can then be treated accordingly. Sometimes Haworthias – particularly the retuse type – lose their fleshy roots. If this occurs, the dead basal leaves should be removed and the rosette placed on top of fresh compost. Usually they will produce new roots within a few weeks.

MESEMBRYANTHEMACEAE

This Family has its greatest concentration in South Africa, though a few species occur as far afield as Australia and South America.

The plants range in size from ½in (12mm) to small shrubs. The degree of succulence also varies, reaching its most extreme in *Lithops*, *Dinteranthus* and *Conophytum* and similar types, whose near-spherical bodies consist of a fused pair of leaves. The daisy-like flowers, which normally open when the sun is at its brightest (hence the popular name 'Midday Flowers'), are often brightly coloured and long-lasting. The familiar 'Livingstone Daisy' used as a summer bedding plant is a member of the Family. The highly succulent types are most popular with collectors and this account will concentrate on these.

Cheiridopsis

The species most likely to be encountered form small clumps containing a few slender leaves. They are sometimes considered to be reluctant to flower, but in a well-lit situation they will produce their colourful flowers. The colour range is appreciable, as suggested by the species names *candidissima* (white), *aurea* (golden-yellow), *cuprea* (copper-red), *carnea* (pink) and *purpurea* (purple).

Conophytum

These plants are often considered to be stemless, though with age many develop into clusters of bodies connected by short stems. The reduction of leaf surface as a strategy to keep water loss to a minimum results in the bodies consisting of a pair of leaves which are replaced annually. In some species, the 'bilobe' types, the leaves are heart-shaped. Others have conical bodies, while in the most extreme forms the leaf-pairs are united into a single spherical body with only a minute slit at the top. Some species have attractively marked bodies, rather similar to but smaller than those of the related *Lithops*.

The growing period is autumn and winter, when new leaves replace those of the previous year and flowers are produced. That done, the plants should be kept dry until they show signs of growth in late summer or early autumn. Usually the 'bilobe' types are the first to start into growth, and they tend to be the most vigorous.

The range of flower colour is considerable, and includes shades of white, yellow, orange, pink, red, copper and magenta. A few, flowering at night, have pale flowers and are pleasantly scented, presumably to attract pollinators. The flowers are produced from between the two leaves and often every head produces a flower.

With around four hundred names published, the choice available to the collector is wide and none will disappoint. Some will be attracted by the body form and colour, others by the flowers. Among the 'bilobe' types, *Conophytum bilobum* has heart-shaped green leaves edged with red and freely produces golden-yellow flowers. *Conophytum frutescens* has a shrubbier habit and orange flowers. *Conophytum notabile* has bluish-green leaves and coppery flowers.

Conophytum obconellum has flat-topped conical bodies, from which whitish perfumed flowers are produced. *Conophytum scitulum* has bodies of similar shape, but their tops are marked with reddish-brown lines. Its flowers are white. *Conophytum tischeri* has the tops of its bodies marked with green dots and produces purplish-lilac flowers. The bodies of *Conophytum calculus* are almost spherical, with just a tiny slit, and its flowers are yellow. *Conophytum ectypum* var. *ectypum* is a mat-forming plant with roughened tops to the bodies and pink flowers. A very attractive contrast results from the combination of coppery-brown body and white flowers in *Conophytum cupreatum*.

Faucaria

Although this genus contains over thirty species, few are in cultivation. They are short-stemmed, branching plants with chunky leaves often edged with long, soft teeth and giving rise to the popular name 'Tiger Jaws'. Flowers, usually yellow, are produced in late summer and autumn. Faucarias should be grown in gritty compost in full sun to encourage a compact habit.

Faucaria tigrina is the best-known species, with leaves covered with small white dots. *Faucaria tuberculosa* has a similar habit, but the upper sides of the leaves have prominent fleshy

Fig 113 Faucaria tigrina.

tubercles. Although not easy to find, *Faucaria candida* is worth searching for, as it has white flowers.

Frithia

The monotypic genus *Frithia* contains only *Frithia pulchra*, a gem that should be in every collection. It is a small, stemless plant, forming clusters about 1in (2.5cm) in diameter. The leaves are about 5⁄8in (15mm) long, flattened at the tip with a translucent 'window'. The long-lasting flowers, produced during the summer, are usually purple though a white form has been reported. The plants should be grown in a well-drained compost and watered with care.

Lithops

This is undoubtedly the most popular genus in the Family. The plants have a single pair of fleshy leaves, united into a conical body, usually separated by a narrow fissure but occasionally gaping more widely, and terminating in a flattened surface patterned with windows. Most eventually form clumps, but even old specimens rarely exceed 4in (10cm) in diameter. The attraction lies in the range of body colour and patterning. Flowers are produced in late summer and autumn and are white or yellow, though there are subtle variations of shade. There are approximately thirty-five species, many of which have several varieties or forms, providing scope for an attractive collection that can be housed within a small space.

Among the yellow-flowered species *Lithops aucampiae* forms clusters of a few large bodies with slightly rounded tops, brown with darker markings. *Lithops pseudotruncatella* is smaller in size but with a flatter top. Most varieties have greyish bodies and are marked with a network of brownish lines; var. *elisabethiae* has a purplish-pink body but is otherwise similar. *Lithops hookeri*, more likely to be found labelled with

Fig 114 Frithia pulchra.

Fig 115 Lithops aucampiae.

the older name *Lithops turbiniformis*, is another large-bodied form with several varieties. *Lithops lesliei* has the largest area of distribution and in consequence is very variable. Usually the body is brown with darker markings, but sometimes the base colour is greyish. The variety *venteri* is grey with black markings. An unusual form, which has received the cultivar name 'Albinica', is yellowish-green with darker green markings and has white flowers. *Lithops olivacea* has small greyish bodies and large open windows: young plants are often pinkish in colour. *Lithops otzeniana* is one of the most distinctively marked species, with grey body and irregular, scalloped windows which resemble an open mouth with prominent teeth.

The group of white-flowered types contains equally attractive plants. *Lithops julii* and its varieties have grey bodies with darker markings while *Lithops hallii* is brown with dark markings. *Lithops salicola* is a variable species, grey with darker windows which may be large and open or finely divided. *Lithops comptonii* is a pretty species with small, purplish-grey bodies. The most distinctive and naturally the most desirable species is *Lithops optica* cv. 'Rubra', which has purplish-pink bodies and deep ruby-red windows.

Lithops are easy plants to grow once their needs are recognised. A well-drained compost and good light are essential, but it is the watering regime that is most important. The leaf-pair is replaced every year by new leaves which grow while the old ones shrivel. For this to be accomplished correctly, the plants must be kept absolutely dry from the end of the flowering period (early winter) until the new leaves are fully developed, which usually takes until early summer. Watering during this period will halt the drying process and the plants will develop more than one pair of leaves, thus destroying their character.

Pleiospilos

The most attractive members of this genus are those that uncannily resemble pieces of rock.

Fig 116 Titanopsis calcarea.

Pleiospilos bolusii has a pair of large, fleshy, angular leaves, greyish-green and becoming purplish-grey when exposed to bright sunlight. The under-surface is tuberculate while the upper surface is smooth, giving the impression that the plant is a split rock. The deception is revealed when the golden flower appears in the crevice. *Pleiospilos simulans* is somewhat similar, but with a flatter upper surface. *Pleiospilos nelii* has leaves that are more rounded and a yellow to pinkish flower.

To maintain the characteristic shape of these plants it is essential to water sparingly. Given too much water, they become bloated, even splitting, and produce additional leaves.

Titanopsis

The best-known species is *Titanopsis calcarea*, so named for its occurrence on limestone and for the way it resembles that material. In the habitat the plant forms tight cushions with only the leaf-tips exposed, and these are covered with whitish warts, causing the plant to resemble a piece of limestone and presumably affording some protection from predators. It is difficult to achieve such compact growth in cultivation, but a well-lit situation and sparse watering will prevent the plant from losing too much of its character. The flowers are yellow to orange and just less than 1in (2.5cm) in diameter.

CHAPTER 7

Moving On

MORE DIFFICULT PLANTS

Throughout this book, reference has been made to some plants being more difficult to cultivate than others, and so it is advisable to delay their acquisition until experience has been gained with a broad range of easier types. Purchasing the more difficult kinds is likely to lead to disappointment. Even if they do not die within a short time, they may languish, refusing to grow or flower. As the more difficult types tend also to be more expensive, a few such disappointments may discourage the novice and deny him or her the pleasures of the hobby.

The skill of coping with these difficult plants is normally acquired slowly and sometimes expensively. It is not something which can be distilled from books which, because of the wide range of plants covered, can offer only general advice. Discussing cultural techniques with other growers can be fruitful: most will be flattered and willing to share their experience. Specialist nurseries will also give advice – it is in their interest to establish a good relationship with customers.

If such personal contact is not possible, knowledge of a plant's origin may be helpful. Generally, though not invariably, the plants from warmer areas such as Brazil, tropical America, Arabia, Madagascar and India are likely to be more difficult than those from more temperate regions. Those that have a wide geographical range are usually more accommodating than those from a restricted habitat. Plants with tuberous rootstocks usually require greater care in watering than those with fibrous roots. But remember, these are generalities: there are many exceptions to the general rules!

SHOWING

An interest in succulents often stems from a visit to a show. In Britain, most shows are competitive, with exhibitors vying in a spirit of friendly rivalry for the modest prizes offered. The act of exhibiting one's plants is a natural adjunct to cultivating them, providing an opportunity for them to be measured against those grown by other exhibitors.

The first plunge into the world of showing is one that novices are often reluctant to take, the main concern being that their efforts will be ridiculed by more knowledgeable enthusiasts. Competing for the first time in a specialist show can be daunting. The opposition will include people who have been cultivating and exhibiting plants for many years. It may be better to seek out the general horticultural shows that include a small cactus and succulent section. There the competition will be less fierce – and usually the prize money is greater than in the specialist shows!

It may be helpful to know how succulent plants are judged in specialist shows where qualified judges are almost invariably employed. Basically the judge will be examining the cultural skills of the grower.

The condition of the plant is of prime importance. A worthy exhibit will be of the correct shape, not bloated from over-feeding, shrunken from being kept too dry, etiolated from being grown in a poorly illuminated position, or of an irregular shape induced by an erratic cultural regime. It will have a healthy colour, not showing signs of scorch or cold damage, or unevenness due to deficiency of some essential food ele-

Fig 117 *A collection of cacti.*

Fig 118 Stapelia schinzii.

Fig 119 Neoporteria hankeana.

ment. The plant should be free from such physical damage as missing spine clusters and broken leaves. There should be no signs of pests or diseases, or damage resulting from such attacks.

Maturity is important, as an old plant should always beat a younger one of the same type if their condition is similar. This does not necessarily mean that a large plant will beat a smaller one: the latter may be a more mature specimen of a smaller-growing species. Open flowers are not essential, but if the plant exhibited is of a kind that normally flowers in cultivation, the judge will look for buds, open flowers, floral remains, fruits or even flowering scars as evidence that the plant is performing as expected.

A small amount of credit will be given for difficulty of cultivation, rewarding the exhibitor who is successfully coping with the demands of a species generally reckoned to be difficult to grow. Similarly, a rare plant will receive more credit than a common one. However, rarity and difficulty of cultivation together should not lift a poorly grown specimen above a well-grown example of a common and easy type.

Thought should be given to presenting an entry in such a way as to catch the eye of the judge. A clean container, compost that is free of weeds and algae, perhaps a suitable top-dressing of natural stone chippings or grit, and a neatly written label all enhance the appearance of the plant.

The novice should not be afraid to ask other exhibitors for advice regarding the suitability of a proposed entry: most will respond helpfully. Judges too, if approached after they have completed their deliberations, will explain how they made their decisions. The important thing is to enjoy the show as a social occasion and use it to measure how successfully one is cultivating the plants. Prizes should be a secondary consideration.

IN CONCLUSION

It is hoped that this modest work will persuade those attracted to succulent plants, but fearful that their exotic appearance signifies difficulty in cultivation, that it is possible to grow a healthy, free-flowering collection with a minimum of trouble. Those teetering on the brink are encouraged to take up the hobby: they have nothing to lose but their hearts!

Index

Note: The page numbers of illustrations are indicated in *italic* type.